THE POWER OF MANAGEMENT CAPITAL

THE POWER OF MANAGEMENT CAPITAL

Utilizing the New Drivers of Innovation, Profitability, and Growth in a Demanding Global Economy

Armand V. Feigenbaum
President and CEO
General Systems Company, Inc.

AND

Donald S. Feigenbaum
Executive Vice President and COO
General Systems Company, Inc.

McGraw-Hill
New York Chicago San Francisco Lisbon
London Madrid Mexico City Milan New Delhi
San Juan Seoul Singapore Sydney Toronto

The McGraw·Hill Companies

Copyright © 2003 by The McGraw-Hill Companies, Inc. All rights reserved. Printed in the United States of America. Except as permitted under the United States Copyright Act of 1976, no part of this publication may be reproduced or distributed in any form or by any means, or stored in a data base or retrieval system, without the prior written permission of the publisher.

1 2 3 4 5 6 7 8 9 0   DOC/DOC   0 9 8 7 6 5 4 3

ISBN 0-07-021733-5

RR Donnelley was printer and binder.

This book is printed on acid-free paper.

Management Capital is a service mark of the General Systems Company. The Power of Management Capital and Management Capital are trade names of the General Systems Company.

Contents

Preface vii

1 New Management for Business Growth in a Demanding Economy 1

2 Capitalizing Management Power: Lessons from the Great Japanese Economy 17

3 Emphasizing Quality of Management Instead of Quantity of Management 35

4 The Character of the Company: "Signature" Capabilities and Management Innovation 57

5 Managing for Growth in the New Competitive Landscape 73

6 Sustaining Business Growth by Recognizing and Reconnecting Management "Disconnects" 89

7 Reducing Failure Costs and Increasing Systems Effectiveness 113

8 Developing Visible and Invisible Competitive Strength and "Materializing" Management Capital 135

9 Ten Leadership Characteristics for Capitalizing Management Power throughout the Business Value Chain 155

10 **The Customer—Not Wall Street—Delivers the Business's Income** 175

11 **Powering Management Capital** 189

Index 193

Preface

THE OPENING YEARS OF THE TWENTY-FIRST century have been an incubator of great opportunities for businesses that understand and respond to their new marketplaces and global requirements. However, this period has been a shattering experience for companies that have been slow to recognize and deal with the fundamental changes in the economic and social demands that have created these opportunities.

The results are reflected in the significant variation among the profitability and growth patterns of businesses in numerous industries. Many companies have continued to develop as powerful agents of business improvement. Some, however, have declined in growth and profitability. Still others, unfortunately, seem to have become sandboxes for financial leveraging.

Two areas of overriding corporate emphasis have emerged from this brutally competitive economy. The first is a fundamentally new character of business innovation. The second is a powerfully new focus on the carry-over business issues from the expansive economy of the 1990s and the early twenty-first century.

Pacesetter companies both large and small are generally quite aware of this. These pacesetters are the organizations that consistently, relentlessly, and successfully recognize, emphasize, and utilize competitively strong new ways of deploying and integrating their companies' total resources in new and more effective category-breaker ways to seize today's strong business opportunities.

A NEW CHARACTER OF BUSINESS INNOVATION

Among the several examples of this new character of business innovation is a new, much more effective, and fully business-integrated utilization of technology resources for broad company competitive leadership. This is very different from the self-contained islands of technology that once characterized some organizations. These broad twenty-first-century developments in and impacts of technology are built into and directly integrated across all product and service development in a company and throughout all operations, marketing, and distribution areas as a fundamental competitive leadership strategy. In this sense, today's Wal-Mart, with its recognition, development, purchase, and utilization of digitized operations for results throughout its merchandising business, can be thought of as being almost as much a technology company as Microsoft is.

The increasingly better development and positioning of brand names and branding in an increasing number of companies is another significant although not yet as widely recognized example. When consistently developed and understood and effectively coordinated, strong focusing of company brands has been creating results that align a business's character throughout the entire organization in new and powerful ways. It greatly improves recognition by customers and can significantly assist sales. Again, it does not unduly stretch business judgment to recognize that today's technology companies, such as Intel, have long been moving toward the business effectiveness of brand recognition and selling almost to the same degree as merchandisers such as Coca Cola and Pepsi.

A further example of this powerful way to gain market share is the focus on designing, producing, and selling products and services with strategically dominant quality leadership integrated with conformance to the same technical standards and practices as those used by competitors. Toyota's strength in the automotive industry is one instance of this.

WHAT MAKES THIS WORK

Underlying this business leadership strength has been the gradual but nonetheless significant shift both in the content of business investments and in the way they are managed.

It is evidenced in the gradual but enormous shift in the character of investment in the assets that drive business results and competitiveness. U.S. nonfinancial corporations' investment in tangible "hard" assets—brick and mortar, equipment, and inventories—has been gradually dropping from more than three-quarters of the total to slightly over one-half.

This increase has occurred in investment in intangible "soft" assets: copyrights, patents, and the many other forms of intellectual assets. To give just a few examples, this includes a fully connected direct management leadership focus on a company's customer relationships, human resources, and supplier integration as well as the previously mentioned technology, brands, and quality.

This has been progressively changing the character and meaning and the skills and tools of successful leadership and management. It has strikingly increased the importance of the effectiveness of those elements in the integration of soft and hard assets throughout the infrastructure and e-frastructure of today's successful companies. It has an important effect on the content and positioning and the overview of corporate governance.

Two basic characteristics stand out in the companies that are most successful in these terms: their quality of management and what we have come to call their management capital.

The *quality of management* involves the leadership passion, the populism, and the disciplined responsibility for sustaining and accelerating a business's growth and profitability, particularly in the following ways:

- Customer value leadership, including product and service development that create a lock on the future
- Operating cost leadership for the company's economic strength
- Management innovation and total resource use for competitive business improvement
- Empowering a company culture of superior performance

Management capital is a business's overarching theme for effectively recognizing, developing, accumulating, deploying, and measuring the capacity and effectiveness of the company's total resources—hard assets as well as soft—to accomplish these results in sustaining and accelerating growth and profitability.

One of the primary characteristics of this new twenty-first-century management is its meaning and emphasis concerning innovation. This is characterized by the institutionalization of—and the infrastructure and integration for—constant *management* innovation, which is also a necessary condition for successful product and service research and development. The reason for this is that today the emphasis of a successful business innovation in pacesetter companies is that it also positions a company for the next innovation: It is not just an end in itself.

CLEAR FOCUS ON CARRYOVER BUSINESS ISSUES FROM THE RECENT PAST

Implementing these innovative actions and steps to take advantage of today's opportunities also brings into very sharp focus for today's companies the carryover business demands from the very different environment that characterized much of business during the decade of the 1990s and into the very recent past. Throughout those years a rising sea of expansion was created by a combination of abundant resource availability, regulatory easing, strong technological growth, and acquisitions, mergers, and alliances. It was an era of high customer demand and expectations with both consumer and business willingness to spend money to support those expectations.

Many markets were clearly sellers' markets both because of strong household and corporate buyer income levels and because of the successful development and marketing of products and services ranging from innovative technology for industrial companies to conspicuous consumption products and services for consumers. Many of those products and services commanded high volume, strong pricing, and the corresponding top-line growth and significant profitability. Business and management practices responded to and were heavily defined in these growth and expansionist terms in that period.

While a great deal of the management strength of this recent past remains important, today's business leadership is characterized by no longer depending unduly on similarly very good markets or on single technological silver bullets as some companies had done to achieve strong business results.

This type of leadership does not accept some past judgments that confused the results of a very strong economy with assumptions about strong management practices.

To give just some of the better-known examples, the issues from these practices can include the following:

- The aftereffects of the focus on short-term stock price increases sometimes more than on a superior return on the financial capital invested in the business, including its acquisitions
- The lower sales results from having pursued marketing trends with me-too products that provided very little bottom-line advantage or longer-term customer sales positioning

- The economic consequences of the mergers and acquisitions that created balance sheet difficulties because they delivered no new combination of competitive strengths and little or no new business value to the acquirer

Today's pacesetting business leaders focus on eliminating the resulting disconnects—that is, the breaks and ambiguities within the company's management infrastructure—and on measuring and eliminating the business failure costs that are their consequence.

A fundamental and effective process and discipline of corporate governance is a key dimension of this.

WHY WE WROTE THE BOOK AND ITS PLAN

Our purpose in writing this book was to discuss our experience in achieving these innovational business improvement results based on General Systems Company's work in helping our customer companies in the United States and throughout the world sustain and accelerate their profitability and growth. The book is written from the authors' perspective of many years of hands-on experience and know-how in helping to accomplish these improvement results. And as part of our initiative to help and guide companies in profitability and growth, we have also been continually studying the performance characteristics of those with whom we have not been directly involved.

The Power of Management Capital is directed to the men and women in organizations, large and small, who are responsible for or involved with the drivers of increasingly successful performance ranging from emphasis on this new character of business innovation to the clear focus on the carryover business issues. The book's emphasis is on the application of new ways to improve results in today's enormously demanding and brutally competitive economic, social, political, and international environment.

The book was designed and written to express and recognize the modern field of management as a body of leadership, technological, behavioral, economic, and multinational knowledge. Modern management's application and value extend today far beyond their original emphasis in industrial business operations, although of course they remain fundamental there. Their importance is now also recognized as essential in organizational performance ranging from education, government, and medicine to international bodies and technology.

There are 11 chapters that are integrated and coordinated so that together they convey the full focus and applications of *The Power of Management Capital*, such as the following:

- Understanding of the tectonic shift in the character of business investment in profit-driving assets and in the management of those assets for strong business results
- Systematic identification of the key opportunities for accomplishing those business results
- Leadership for exorcising outworn twentieth-century management doctrines and replacing them with new and more powerful practices to meet those new opportunities and demands
- Clear identification and effectiveness assurance of major management capital channels for creating and delivering those results, including their digitization where appropriate
- Recognition of management capital tools and measurements for accomplishing those results
- Effective management capital structuring, certainly recognizing the importance of clear corporate governance
- Consistent delivery of results for company stakeholders, including an emphasis on the fact that the customer—not Wall Street—delivers a company's income

The book was written so that each chapter can be read for its particular purposes and its impact on current opportunities and demands.

To make the book as relevant as possible, business experience that has been widely reported is used in places where it can be helpful and productive. Some of the instances appear in Chapter 5's discussion of *alliances, technology,* and *digitized management innovation opportunity*.

To provide maximum information for the reader, especially about the scope and substance of the management capital improvement processes themselves, sections termed "Examples" are organized and written together with the accompanying figures. They are representative of a group and type of generic management capital experience with composites of data from General Systems and other sources and are not intended to identify the performance of a specific company or organization.

ACKNOWLEDGMENTS

For the authors to express their debt and appreciation to those who have influenced this book, they would have to list scores of individuals in their own company—unfortunately too numerous to name—whose work has helped over a long period to create and build what management capital represents and what it stands for. Our gratitude is very deep to the many men and women—again too many to name—in the customer companies with which General Systems has worked for their help and their friendship and for how much they have taught us.

We want to express our deep appreciation to Ms. Leslie Warren for preparing and overseeing completion of the manuscript and for personally administering key areas of its process.

We also want to thank our publisher, Philip Ruppel, for his guidance with a lightness of touch and for his patience; Mrs. Nora Frederick for her development of all figures and graphic art; and, Ms. Ruth Mills for her editorial assistance.

Armand V. Feigenbaum
Donald S. Feigenbaum
General Systems Company
Pittsfield, Massachusetts

THE POWER OF MANAGEMENT CAPITAL

CHAPTER 1

NEW MANAGEMENT FOR BUSINESS GROWTH IN A DEMANDING ECONOMY

WHICH FACTORS HAVE DRIVEN the strong business growth of pacesetter companies in the United States and throughout the world? How can companies renew and sustain those factors in the face of the business slowdowns and major fluctuations that challenge the long-term continuation of profitable earnings?

As we continue to experience the twenty-first century's economic, social, and political churning, how will these driving factors be influenced by the brutally competitive global economy in which organizations do not have any particular geographic identity or travel under any particular national passport? What will be the effect of the rapid gyrations in markets that emphasize the difficulties that accounting practices face in determining true performance costs and that forecasting programs confront in establishing the economic determinants of corporate planning? In addition to these challenges, many analytical and strategic evaluation approaches that are used in an attempt to identify and project how well a company is performing have been overwhelmed by the frequency and magnitude of these economic groundswells. In today's competitive climate, where the changes *outside* a business exceed the productive changes *within* a business, a company's future viability is clearly under enormous stress.

To maintain business growth and a sustained economy, it is essential for managers to understand and find solutions for these and other fundamental wide-ranging issues. The bursting of the high-tech bubble both in many start-up companies and in major segments of established firms dissipated many entrepreneurial efforts and the large sums of money that were spent to create organizations that never earned a profit and were often hugely unsuccessful as business entities. However, this enormous cost to some companies also created beneficial impacts for many other companies in dealing with these fundamental wide-ranging issues. These beneficial impacts had an enormous effect in galvanizing fundamental business innovation in companies at a far faster rate than would have been the case if there had been no boom; that is, without those effects, innovation might not have taken place at all.

All this business growth has caused increasing complexity in business action and decision making. It has presented chief executive officers (CEOs) and management leaders in all markets and industries with new intricacies in deciding how to weigh and time the business decisions—and the quality of those decisions—that increasingly challenge their companies' basic survival.

THE DEMANDS OF SUSTAINING PROFITABLE GROWTH IN A BUSINESS ENVIRONMENT WHERE THE FAST DEVOUR THE SLOW

Our work in helping to increase the profitability of many of the world's major companies (as well as our database surveys of many other companies) has made it clear that all this complexity has been changing the fundamental dimensions of business strategy and the meaning of its implementation. These changes affect a broad range of decisions, including the following:

- How to invest in technology
- How to lead meaningful human resources initiatives
- How to maintain alliances successfully
- What the speed of new product or service development should be
- What the appropriate time horizons for investments and financial planning are
- How to implement productive cost reduction
- How to recognize when regular audits of quality compliance will not guarantee customer loyalty

Businesses are growing more intricate and at warp speed. For example, consider the effects of venture capital financing, multiple marketing channel distribution, and entirely new patterns of employee recruiting, development, and training. In addition, product and services launches increasingly require more effective development initiatives. Rapidly increasing numbers of new offerings—from Web-oriented modules to credit cards—are being commoditized in months or even weeks instead of the periods of years on which companies had counted for cash flow.

Increasingly demanding consumer and industrial buyers are basing their purchasing decisions on the *quality* of products and services, and this requires manufacturers to be vastly more effective and to strengthen the way they manage customer relationships. The sellers are now deeply partnered with supply chain processes; this means that the cost and timing of new product releases have taken on new meaning and have new requirements.

Fixed costs, which have always been a fundamental factor in managing profit maintenance and growth during fluctuations in the economy, have taken on additional management dimensions, especially for technology products, in which variable costs become low. An example is software, for which production costs can be minimal. When customers may suddenly cut back on their purchases, the traditional emphasis on reducing variable costs to achieve profit maintenance is not likely to be very effective. The competitive necessity to maintain high levels of development, with the corresponding high levels of fixed costs, can accelerate cycles and up-and-down fluctuations in profitability as those fixed costs remain firm, therefore requiring different approaches to innovation in management.

This is a world where even in established disciplines such as economics some of the founding principles, such as Adam Smith's "invisible hand," are being tested and reworked for the first time in more than 200 years. The traditional basic premise of volume production, which has driven manufacturing for decades—primarily economies of scale—is being challenged by today's reality.

Continuing with the example of software, once a successful software development has been created, the cost of volume production is almost nothing, and a company can maintain its market dominance until it is challenged *not* by economies of scale but by being shoved aside by the next temporarily dominant product. This is changing the whole concept of manufacturing and factories in some industries.

RECOGNIZING THE IMPORTANCE OF THE *QUALITY* OF PRODUCTIVITY

Underlying many of these conditions is the Internet (now almost universally understood as multipurpose technology), which has the potential to help define business effectiveness both in the creation of *new products* and in terms of *new productivity*. This goes well beyond digitizing businesses. Instead, it confronts established companies with basic demands for innovation that extend far beyond technology, particularly in terms of how to traverse the Net's business plan minefields. Moreover, it confronts the more durable and surviving dot-com businesses with equally basic issues of innovation in regard to making their *fiscal discipline* as focused as their *market development*.

Productivity, which has always been recognized as a primary driver of prosperity and profitability, has been widely emphasized as a continuing key to this economic strength. It has been discussed quite properly in terms of the rapid growth of technology, particularly information technology. However, in these times when the fast devour the slow, productivity also particularly relates to the significance of the ways in which a company can maintain its fundamental business innovation as a key to its competitive leadership and as a necessary condition for the profitability and effectiveness of technology.

Today another economic force—the *quality* of productivity—is being recognized as essential for shoring up the economy, especially when business slows down. From SUVs and computers to Internet services and home furnishings, the *quality value* that buyers perceive in products and services is becoming an enormously powerful influence on the continuing strength of customer spending, especially when times are tight.

Study of the current economy indicates that when today's consumer is completely satisfied with his or her product or service purchase, he or she tells six other potential buyers. In contrast, a *dissatisfied* consumer informs 25 other potential buyers. That is the leverage of quality in shaping consumer sentiment, which is vital in powering the two-thirds of the American economy that is consumer-driven. Therefore, as companies again go back to the business basics, this is a reminder of the most fundamental of those basics: Company managers need to recognize that a business's income comes from its *customers,* not from Wall Street.

NEW LEADERSHIP AND NEW MANAGEMENT MODELS ARE REQUIRED TO MEET THE BREADTH OF NEW CUSTOMER DEMANDS

Most management leaders fully understand that the one certainty in the volcanic twenty-first-century economy is that the terrain on which their businesses will operate tomorrow will be shaped differently from the terrain of today. They recognize that the business requirement is to lead accordingly, and they know that this type of leadership requires an understanding of the characteristics of the business initiatives that can meet the demands for supporting strong earnings growth in turbulent market conditions.

Our work has shown that new powers of leadership and management are becoming a *seminal force* in creating the various initiatives for meeting the breadth of these demands in companies that have become pacesetters. The impact of these powers will be a strong force in governing the way business operates during the next years of the twenty-first century. Pacesetter companies are succeeding by means of a leadership attitude characterized by firm financial responsibility to customers, investors, employees, and other stakeholders. This leadership attitude and orientation simultaneously focuses on the rewards and risks of the opportunistic growth, the immense potential of human resource effectiveness, and the speed of action required for success in today's demanding competitive climate.

Furthermore, the competitive climate is not a war of so-called Old Economy versus New Economy concepts. Instead, the competitive climate involves the *convergence* of the management models that have been proved to work best in both throughout today's marketplace. Business leaders need to understand that the current marketplace is characterized by the following business truths:

- The quick and most flexible devour the ponderous and most rigid.
- Networking and diffusion work better than bureaucracy does.
- An emphasis on creativity is essential.
- The people closest to what is happening are those who can lead and improve it the most effectively for a sustained economy.

As communication has become increasingly less expensive, it has become more and more productive to provide access for all employees to the information that can help them make their own decisions as well as the authority to make those decisions.

RECOGNIZING THE IMPORTANCE OF THE *QUALITY* OF MANAGEMENT

Company leadership builds this new business effectiveness as it systematically develops, operates, measures, and integrates all of the following things:

- Market and leadership capabilities
- Technology capacities
- Brand names
- Customer relationships
- Human resources
- International connections
- Business processes
- Supply networks
- Quality and service capability

Moreover, all these factors must be considered in the context of a business's all-important *physical assets* and *financial capital*. These two factors have been the primary "hard-asset" business emphasis that was the focus of the executive management of some of the companies that dominated certain Old Economy markets. Those managers viewed "soft-asset" capabilities as intangibles that were more appropriate for "staff" and support work.

For those businesses, a company's management strength usually was judged and measured by the depth and capability and hard-asset credentials of the company's management. That, of course, remains critically important. However, American companies whose performance most readily slipped in the economic crucible at the beginning of the twenty-first century (and whose recovery was among the slowest) seemed to rate highest in hard-asset terms compared with the many companies with a higher mix of soft-asset management strength, whose results were far better. Today's pacesetter companies no longer view their management strength in those terms of an earlier day.

In contrast to companies that emphasize hard assets, *pacesetter companies* emphasize a *quality-of-management* approach that is recognized and measured in terms of the know-how for relentlessly focusing and integrating a company's full resources—soft as well as hard—in the new management and leadership models with a competitively strong infrastructure for sustaining its business growth. This is also the foundation for connecting with the "e-frastructure" of the Internet for the productivity and sales growth value of e-commerce and e-business. This quality-of-management emphasis is particularly critical in times like these, which combine unusual growth opportunities with the problems of significant business disconnects created by long economic expansions.

The business importance of all this is that because of today's brutally competitive customer markets, these *total* (i.e., hard assets as well as soft assets) capacities are the competitive strengths through which pacesetters bring together the kinds of customer product and services value packages whose sale creates the kind of business-building, full-satisfaction customer experience that develops loyalty and repeat business. This integration of total capacities is the key to sustaining profitability today. Pacesetter companies are increasingly moving to manage and lead their organizations in these terms.

For example, consider the continuously strong performance of long-term business powerhouses as diverse as General Electric, Union Pacific, and Wal-Mart. Moreover, the successful confluence of this kind of management with technology sends a similar message when one gets equally deeply into highly fluctuating markets and businesses ranging from Intel to

Dell. This has also been a basis for the resurgence of great technology-driven corporations such as IBM from the severe down cycles it had experienced. This marriage of leadership and technology capability can also be credited for the success of E-Bay.

Some astute investors and managers long ago figured out this power of management capital in establishing their valuations of growth companies—and with lucrative results in terms of the principle that an indicator of the value of a company is the sum of its *brand name* and its *management* systems.

THE CHARACTER OF LEADERSHIP NECESSARY FOR SUCCESS AT PACESETTER COMPANIES

The profitability and growth of pacesetter companies is driven by a type of leadership that has the passion, populism, and disciplined responsibility to understand and effectively manage the *total* resources and relationships that form the foundation of the broadly based business value of the twenty-first-century company. Such leadership is also a necessary condition for a company's success in e-business and e-commerce and in realizing the Internet's potential for strong product growth as well as effective productivity growth.

This profitability and growth means superiority in the business leadership effectiveness of a company's physical, financial, and other assets that were once the primary management emphasis. This profitability and growth also entails their integration with the effectiveness of a company's human strengths, customer and supplier relationships, brand names and technology, and smarts of knowledge and intellect. Most important, this profitability and growth means the successful implementation of these leading-edge initiatives in hands-on organization wide actions that provide measurable competitive advantage on a continuing basis.

Such management leadership has long had many powerful business pacesetting examples, ranging from the meritocracy form of organization that was a key to the early success of the information technology industry (from chips to computers) to the just-in-time and lean production management concepts that helped restore American manufacturing strength from the origination in Japan of some of its current practices. This kind of leadership has not always been widely recognized as a fundamental productivity key to expansive business growth over the last several years. Such improvement initiatives often are not fully quantified. However, they collectively represent much of the competitive capability of today's companies and must be managed accordingly. Correspondingly, in pacesetter companies the importance of this kind of leadership is emphasized. This is a fundamentally different situation from what once was the often not very productive intermittent emphasis on these "intangible" and "soft" assets by "fireworks displays" of emphasis primarily on the part of corporate staff groups that have long since been downsized in many companies.

THE WAY THE COMPANY WORKS: A NEW COMPETITIVE ADVANTAGE

Pacesetter companies develop these powers of management by changing the focus of their leadership. In the last several years there has been an increasing and relentless emphasis on the *form, frequency,* and *scope* of leadership for establishing superiority in the way a company works throughout all aspects of its organization and its customer, supplier, relationship, and alliance networks. These leaders have focused on ensuring that the *way* a company works in all areas is the competitive driver that sustains that company's *profitable growth* and becomes the *invisible strength* that competitors find hard to understand and duplicate. These leaders also focus on the measurements that make it clear that their companies have achieved these goals. This focus is fundamentally different from the traditional business focus on trying to make a business career of unduly specialized strength in a few operational areas.

Leaders who focus on *the customer marketplace* recognize and manage the implementation of this business principle because they realize that it is a necessary precondition and platform for the success of their businesses' products and services—*not* vice versa, as in some companies. In addition, corporate pacesetter leaders not only recognize this, they also have the know-how for implementing it: They know it is the primary basis for a company's profitability strength. This is how they have outdistanced their competitors, who have not quite figured out that this is key to a company's competitive advantage.

Examples abound of the power of this kind of business strength:

- GE was one of the pioneers. It implemented the idea of the boundaryless organization, the practice of delayering, and the policy of one-or-two-or-out market leadership. Each of these changes was part of the early process and measurement and leadership innovation that accelerated General Electric's competitive power and helped elimi-

nate a hallowed corporate name such as Westinghouse from its New York Stock Exchange listing.
- Another great example is Dell, which implemented leading-edge innovations such as direct-to-customer production sales and supply chain leadership. These innovations allowed Dell to build its computer business volume and success by blindsiding the industry's existing marketing, production, and retailing practices.
- IBM's approach to emphasizing services and partnering with other technology companies—and making it work—has been the key to its strength.
- Our own total quality management (which identified the costs of quality failure and converted them into opportunity improvement) helped Union Pacific further build its profitability strength and leadership. Part of its emphasis is that process management means not merely *process* improvement but fundamental improvement involving entirely *better ways of working*. It recognizes that what one *measures* effectively, one is most likely to *lead and manage* effectively.
- Intel's emphasis on new work flow forms of development and operation triggered fundamental explosions in the way information technology is successfully created and produced.
- Toyota's emphasis on management processes that solve small problems quickly—fully as much as they solve large ones—has provided it with an enormous competitive advantage in one of the world's most demanding industries.

RESULTS FROM INFORMATION TECHNOLOGY AND FROM "DIGITIZING" THE BUSINESS

Moreover, a basic differentiating factor in the leadership of many pacesetter companies has been their recognition of and emphasis on the idea that *systematic*—not casual or intermittent—integration with fundamentally based leading-edge management processes is a necessary condition for the long-term business results of information technology. These leaders understand that by far the most important single reason for the failure of information technology installations that have not fulfilled their intended results has been that this effective *integration* with management innovation has not been implemented.

Today's leaders in digitizing their businesses recognize that information technology generates its *full* economic power only when the effectiveness of that *technological* capability is combined with the effectiveness of a company's customer and business *leadership* capability and the realism of its *marketing and financial discipline*. That also has been one of the primary messages of the selective winners (and the many losers) in the e-business and e-commerce markets and of the continuing drive of successful companies from Amazon to E-Bay.

The business message from all this experience is that the breadth of relentless business and management innovation is a basic key to technology value creation in companies. This key consists of leadership emphasis on the management principle that by digitizing a flawed process, all one does is enable that flawed process to operate faster.

THE DRIVERS OF BUSINESS GROWTH: "GENERAL-PURPOSE" TECHNOLOGY AND SHAPING NEW MANAGEMENT

The powerful results of the American business economy through the end of the 1990s continued to defy and fundamentally challenge many of the traditional approaches regarding how corporate growth and earnings could be predicted and realized—and continue to do so as the economic winds have shifted. Very few longer-term projections got it right—except on a rearview-mirror basis—on either a national or a global basis, and there are several reasons for this.

Of fundamental importance was the fact that the impact of these new leadership and management models, as well as the business innovation they provided, was not always readily recognized or measured. It was Alan Greenspan who early identified its connection with the new explosion of technology (particularly information technology) as a principal force in creating the new business ideas underpinning this economic strength of the United States, with strong levels of productivity and the impact on low inflation establishing new conditions.

This had been the case with the earlier technology explosions, such as electricity, communications, and transportation, which had also changed the American economic environment. These can best be described as "general-purpose" technologies, the creators both of productivity growth and of new products themselves.

Today information technology is this kind of "general-purpose" technology. For example, car and truck companies now use information technology as the basis for the telematics of the communications products installed for driver and passenger use in their cars and trucks and for the management of their supply chains. Like earlier transforming technologies such as electricity and radio, information technology is a foundation both for *creating* new products and services and for establishing new ways to *manage* them. Managing these technologies encourages and requires complementary organizational investments such as new business processes and work practices.

This is also important to companies that are using Internet technology to improve manufacturing by moving away from the traditional production "push" pattern (with its high inventories and long customer delivery times) and toward the far more efficient customer "pull" pattern (which greatly improves these results).

In contrast to the earlier technologies that established the American economy, however, information and the Internet have been bringing an additionally powerful value to business growth. They have increasingly changed the shape of twenty-first-century management and leadership itself, and this change has been demonstrated in the following ways:

- The fast, fact-based decision-making managerial support power of information technology
- The faster-paced, less bureaucratic results provided in both Intranet and Internet forms for self-organizational individual actions within a company's infrastructure
- The fact that connecting the company with the Web's e-frastructure can be so strong a power for both e-commerce and e-business—for example, by creating buyer "self-service" for both sales growth, by increasing customer satisfaction in consumer as well as industrial markets, and by developing supply chain networks that provide breakthrough improvement in procurement

In the last few years companies have learned a great deal about the need for effective new management of this electronic information technology [beyond their earlier experience in their electronic data interchange (EDI) and enterprise resource planning (ERP) and Intranet installations] and what it has taken to achieve real business results from them. They have become very practical about the demand for integration of administrative and technical processes. They also recognize the kind of innovative management it now takes to achieve strong, on-schedule, genuinely high return-on-investment results from electronic information without first having to pass through a period of badly missed schedules where the primary output is that one gets only *more* low-integrity data *faster* than before. This experience has been clarifying how these management innovations have been necessary conditions for information and Internet technology to generate sustainable business results.

MANAGEMENT INNOVATION CAN INCREASE BUSINESS GROWTH

To put these basic forces for American economic growth into perspective, it is essential to recognize that this innovation in business management and leadership over the last decade has in itself become a fundamental business force in providing enormous new impact on American economic growth. For example, consider the following improvements:

- "Lean" production
- Total quality management
- The Silicon Valley meritocracy form of organization
- Emphasis on the individual and on ideas rather than on hierarchy
- Structuring a business in terms of owning only what it does best and partnering and creating alliances for everything else
- Global integration in which components can be shipped from country to country for manufacturing purposes before final production
- Corporate emphasis on an organization's intellectual strength

All these factors are just some of the management innovations that have been basic drivers of productivity and profitability growth.

Figure 1 shows data from our company's experience with the strong results of such business management innovation throughout a wide range of areas—from product development, supply chain, customer relations, and total quality to human resources, alliances, and partnering initiatives—over the last several years and across a wide range of industry segments in many of the major manufacturing and services throughout the world. Measured in terms of actual financial return and actual cost, each bullet within the pattern reflects the performance of specific installations.

Leading-edge pacesetter companies are paying increasing attention to systematically bringing the measuring and reporting of the return on investment (ROI) of this management innovation (and this ROI can often be very rapid) into the measurement and reporting discipline of their long and well-established accounting and finance systems. This rapid ROI is also an indi-

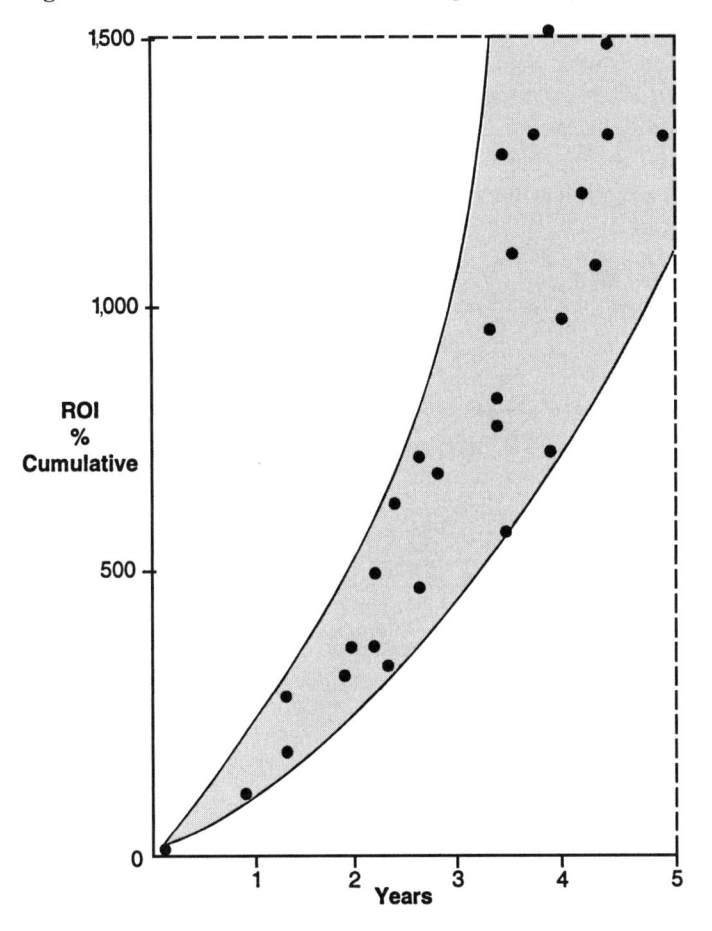

Figure 1 Return on Investment Management Capital Results

cator of the effectiveness of the top corporate leadership and management role in such innovation as it networks and spreads throughout a company. For example, General Electric has systematically measured and widely reported on the strong business results of major innovations such as its work-out and six sigma initiatives. Similarly, Union Pacific reported on the powerful business results of innovations such as its total quality and quality cost initiatives.

This emphasis on management innovation is sharply different from the predominantly hard-asset business pattern of just a few years ago, which was discussed earlier in this chapter and is still embedded in some companies. Companies that focused on hard assets usually regarded investments in management innovations as "soft" because they were based on what traditionally accounting regarded as "intangibles"; that is, they were not explicitly related to brick-and-mortar or physical equipment facilities. These improvement initiatives were measured far less seriously and were not publicly reported by companies.

This emphasis on business management innovation continues to develop rapidly as profitable and growing information technology companies continue to converge in their management practices with strong, profitable, and growing industrial, manufacturing, and services companies as well as health-care companies and consumer products businesses. This emphasis on management innovation also becomes more pervasive as the best results of the implementation of what was once called the "New Economy" approach to management and leadership (which was viewed as "diffused and networked") *converge* with today's payoffs in "Old Economy" companies (which once were thought of as being "hierarchical" and "appointed"). The common denominator is constantly improving the *perceived value* for customers, investors, employees, suppliers, and the public, which is the foundation for success in serving today's very buyer-savvy markets.

Understanding the new strength of business management innovation—and the leadership emphasis that energizes its effects for sustaining growth—is therefore one of the fundamental demands for business structuring and the new management and leadership models that drive it as a company moves forward into the twenty-first century.

CHAPTER 2

CAPITALIZING MANAGEMENT POWER: LESSONS FROM THE GREAT JAPANESE ECONOMY

CHAPTER 1 DISCUSSED THE CHARACTERISTICS of the new strength of business management innovation and its effects on sustaining growth. This chapter discusses the explicit influence of that innovation on the sustained performance of national economies. It also describes how "capitalizing" the management power to accomplish such innovation has caused major changes in the leadership and management of twenty-first-century pacesetter companies.

ECONOMIC EFFECTS OF MANAGEMENT INNOVATION

The effects of innovation have long been recognized as a principal determinant of economic growth, and in recent years the importance of management innovation has become one of the principal factors in that determinant. While difficult to quantify and measure, its results are recognized as one of the most significant influences on economic performance and on the indicators of its results. Some of the globally best known indicators range from the Nikkei 225 Index—of course one of the popular business equity indicators of the performance of principal areas of Japan's economy—to the Dow-Jones Index, one of the principal equity indicators of the American economy.

In the 1980s, which was an era of richly deserved and increasing business leadership for Japan, the Nikkei 225 Index grew significantly. During that period planeloads of American and other Western managers visited Japan to learn the continuing innovation power of "Japanese management" compared with that in much of the United States and the West. Such innovative management in all its forms was clearly recognized as fundamental in powering Japan's increasing world leadership in industries ranging from automobiles to consumer electronics.

As those Japanese innovations became better known throughout the United States and the West, they spread across many companies, with very powerful favorable effects on their business strength. They became powerful center points to add to the strong competitive improvement initiatives already under way in those organizations, while the pace of the leading-edge management innovation in Japan seemed to slow. The Nikkei 225 Index began to drop and continued to drop significantly, while increases in various American and Western economic performance indicators reflected corresponding improvements in the economic and business results in some of those regions.

Of course, there are many influences on economic performance indicators, and nobody knows the full accuracy or dimensions of the comparative effects of such management innovation in global terms. Nevertheless, managers and leaders may find that the following factors are relevant as guidelines for planning:

- What were some of the business factors that drove up the Nikkei?
- What were some of the contributors to its enormous fall?
- What are possible remedies for eliminating those contributors?

THE LEGACY OF THE GREAT JAPANESE ECONOMY

During the 1980s Japan had become the international pacesetter in several areas of cutting-edge *technology* and, for a while, of global business *management* innovations that drove the Japanese economy toward world leadership. In many respects this was the legacy of the aptly named Japanese "gods of management": Dr. Toyoda, Mr. Morita of Sony, and the founder of Matsushita, to name just a few. It was the era of innovative management processes that provided business platforms for Japan's growing global leadership. These were management innovations such as lean production, robust product development, team organization, and, as we know from our own experience, eagerly absorbed American imports such as total quality. Important among those innovations was just-in-time management, whose basic concept was originated by a Toyota production engineer, Mr. Ohno, while he was studying the management of overly long manufacturing cycles and, according to legend, perhaps getting the just-in-time idea by observing the delivery every few hours of fresh fruits and vegetables to American supermarkets.

Dr. Toyoda was gracious enough to discuss some aspects of this innovation principle a number of years ago on a long railroad trip from California to Chicago with a group in which one of the authors was included.

The impression received by some of those who participated in the discussion was that the reason why Toyota was first to move successfully on these innovations had something to do with *technical* areas such as machine and design capability, in which Toyota continued to be very strong, but which were also recognized as very strong throughout the global car industry. It also had much to do with the way Toyota thought about, understood, and believed in the nature of its business and the business innovation, management *process* improvement, and the human and teamwork commitment it required.

The company's *full resources*—its human strengths, technology capacities, supplier relationships, quality focus, and customer and brand relationships, together with its considerable physical and financial assets—were brought together into highly powerful *business and management processes* that were themselves (like the products they drove) driven by continuous innovation. Those processes later were given such now-familiar names as lean production, just in time, and other labels, but their basic leadership principle was to compete by means of the discipline of integrating the organization's full assets.

This was competition managed in a way very different from that used in some areas of the global automotive industry's earlier, very powerful *decentralization* discipline, which had tended to separate all these areas into departmentalized "control silos" and the hierarchical structure that supported the system. This approach had powered the success of much of the American and European automotive industry before it began in the 1970s and 1980s to face serious resistance from customers, employees, and investors because of the rapid acceptance of Japanese automotive products. Japan's competitors in Europe and the United States saw the power of Toyota's approach in its product and service automotive packages. Moreover, the global automotive market in the late 1970s and throughout the 1980s increasingly recognized Toyota as a marketplace pacer and a business growth leader. Those competitors gradually adopted much of that approach as a foundation for their *own* revival of profitability in the 1990s and the early twenty-first century.

Similarly, during that period, some of the same global marketplace results were taking place in other industries for similar reasons—for example, in response to innovative integrated process- and product-driven leadership in companies such as Matsushita, Sony, and Toshiba in consumer electronics, Komatsu and Hitachi in heavy equipment, and Honda and others in automotive, to name just a few of those companies. Because of this *management*-driven product technology and business model strength, some economists predicted during that period that Japan would become the global business leader, with the United States second.

That, of course, did not happen, and ultimately the Japan economy fell—and so did the Nikkei 225. There were many possible contributors to this, related to the following issues, to give just a few examples:

- The banking system
- Corporate structures
- Political changes
- An aging population

The temptation in some companies to equate the continuously strong Japanese economy with continuously good Japanese business management also became a factor in all of this. In addition, the tremendous effectiveness of the original corporate leadership was not always institutionalized in ongoing processes for relentless management innovation.

For example, consider total quality an American innovation that became a signature management leadership area for Japan and a deserved marketplace strength that many Japanese companies literally "owned" in their products throughout the 1980s. However, it was American and other Western companies during the 1990s that increasingly became the leading installers of newer developments, such as total quality management, that became important keys to the resurgence of the American and Western business economies even though many Japanese companies—from automobiles to electronics—maintained their customer quality leadership.

Underlying this economic change were two trends. First, much of the powerful original business-driven management discipline that was responsible for Japan's competitive strength was maintained. However, long-term economic expansions create major business disconnects. In some companies the relentless development of new areas of management leadership was not always institutionalized as the fundamental leading edge it had become as a center point for Japanese product and business leadership in global competitiveness. Second, some of the additional global business opportunities that had been created by global expansion were picked up by Japan's global corporate rivals in the very industries in which Japan had been leading.

One of the business lessons of the Japanese experience regarding the importance of the constancy of management innovation is to avoid two of the biggest competitive dangers companies face no matter how strong their technology and product emphasis may be. The first is the danger of becoming too fond of any business leadership initiative no matter how enormously popular it is. Second, companies must be careful about not sticking with those initiatives for too long. The great Japanese companies are certainly not likely to repeat whatever occurrence of this there might have been as they progress in their resurgent innovational growth in the world marketplace in the twenty-first century.

THE CHALLENGE OF BUSINESS MANAGEMENT INNOVATION

There is little misunderstanding about this in pacesetter companies that have been growing by seizing new business opportunities in the twenty-first century while dealing with some issues remaining from the very different environment that characterized some areas of business during the decade of the 1990s and into the recent past.

In some cases these issues have been carryovers from

- A past overriding focus on achieving short-term stock prices
- Mergers and acquisitions that delivered little or no new combination of competitive strength and little or no business value to the acquirer
- Low sales results from having pursued marketing trends with me-too products
- The aftereffects of what the *New York Times* has described as the "Imperial CEO"

An increasing number of business managers who are leading the success of their companies are coming to recognize the basic principle of this competitive experience. This principle is that there is a fundamental difference between the *periodic* inspirational creation of big and important management innovative initiatives that provide leadership for a while (until they become a businesswide standard or are no longer competitively meaningful) and the clear capability of pacesetter companies to generate an *ongoing* stream of competitive leadership business innovation through management systems and processes that can *sustain* continuing growth. Some companies have been good at periodic bursts of the first type, but those companies are often woefully weak in implementing systematic leadership, attitudes, and disciplines for the second type. That is why the strength of such companies as General Electric, Dell, IBM, and Union Pacific, among many others, resides in their emphasis on *continuing* and *further* management innovations beyond the examples discussed here.

Moreover, the discipline that drives innovation in pacesetter companies is built on the experience that major improvements in twenty-first-century businesses involve a better *way* to *run* the business—which, at the same time, also positions a company to find a further better way to run the business.

However, although some companies have been the fixed "stars" in the implementation of competitive leadership, many other companies have tended to be "comets," flashing up and then down again in the business skies as their management competitive strength has burned itself out. In these comet organizations competitive leadership has been more of a case-by-case occurrence—periodic rather than constant—or has varied with different types of managers' personalities instead of being a carefully *systematic* emphasis.

Even in pacesetter companies, as business circumstances are altered or as managers change, the leading-edge competence may die and be buried without an autopsy. Or it may revert to a bureaucratic initiative such as the centralized strategic planning staffs of an earlier day, where some companies placed innovation in the hands of a few specialists instead of diffusing, encouraging, and supporting it throughout the company. That practice can become a body blow to sustaining growth.

Therefore, structuring and systematizing management innovation is not only a principal competitive *opportunity* for business leaders in twenty-first-century companies, it is a *prerequisite* for success. Systematizing management innovation is an overarching theme that should guide corporate action; it is a fundamental way to lead and manage, and it should become a corporate way of life and even a corporate mindset. Systematizing *management* innovation in the twenty-first century is parallel to the systematization of *technology and product development* in the twentieth century. Recall how new product development became a corporate way of life and mindset, in contrast to the traditional "research and development laboratory" or a periodic flash or revelation. *New product development* was one of the leadership success areas that differentiated twentieth-century corporate leaders from their competitors. Similarly, *systematizing management innovation* is the critical success factor for twenty-first-century pacesetter companies.

CAPITALIZING MANAGEMENT POWER: THE CHANGING ATTITUDES

"Capitalizing" and focusing the strength to accomplish the systematization of management innovation have caused major changes in the leadership and management of twenty-first-century pacesetter companies. These changes have affected the *meaning of* as well as the *approach to* and *practice of* leadership and management. Furthermore, these changes have taken place in four predominant areas:

- Attitudes about ways to sustain growth in markets and business opportunities
- Changing concepts of the basic character and total productive capacities of the twenty-first-century company
- Operationalizing these concepts into business practices

- Recognizing the *disciplined responsibility* of an overarching theme—there is no other phrase to describe it—required for success in networking the successful, organizationwide business management innovation that is the consistent driver of this strength

The next sections of this chapter discuss each of these changes in more detail.

NEW ATTITUDES ON HOW TO SUSTAIN GROWTH THROUGH NEW MARKETS AND NEW BUSINESS OPPORTUNITIES

Regarding attitudes, an increasing number of companies have been challenging (or at least redefining) the traditional top-down strategic and operational corporate approach that holds that "we need a good market for us to grow powerfully." Instead, these companies have been moving toward a continuing emphasis on an entirely new spectrum of opportunities that are being created as New and Old Economies connect globally. These opportunities are creating, expanding, and then redefining these companies' markets and the way they bring products and services to those markets. This opportunistic emphasis covers a broad range of possibilities. For example, it encompasses information technology for establishing service markets for engineered and manufactured products. Or it might consist of patenting e-commerce processes as a competitive advantage in themselves. Or it might be a broad-scale partnership initiative for cooperation and alliances with companies that are bitter competitors in some markets, thereby creating new close relationships that were once unthinkable.

These attitudes have become prevalent at such powerful companies as IBM, Nokia, and E-Bay. For example, IBM has redeveloped itself to achieve its current vibrant strength as a multifaceted product and service leader. Nokia has grown from being a focused product company to being a leader in key global technologies. E-Bay has achieved success in leveraging a single business model into multifaceted opportunities.

The attitude in these and many other pacesetter companies has become one that claims that "we'll develop the total competitive capability both internally and through alliances for marketizing these leading-edge opportunities to sustain profitable growth for our company. We'll fully connect our *total* assets and resources for innovating the competitive strength to manage our way through the wide range of business conditions we must expect in today's brutally demanding markets."

These companies also recognize that good markets will of course help. However, they are not going to depend too much on the market alone;

instead, they are making their growth consistently opportunity-driven and long-term, which also makes them as "recession proof" as possible.

CHANGING CONCEPTS REGARDING A COMPANY'S PRODUCTIVE AND MARKETING CAPACITIES

These attitudes lead directly to the second fundamental change in management content, meaning, and practices in leading organizations. Managers are recognizing how the character of the twenty-first-century company is changing, as well as how its total productive and marketing capacities are changing. This recognition is very different from the traditional corporation's concept, which was largely based on hard assets and was primarily hierarchical—a concept that profoundly and positively influenced the structuring of American and global business for several decades.

The new concept is that of a business organization whose business value resides in the way it combines the power of "tangible hard assets"—its financial assets, equipment, and bricks and mortar—with what used to be thought of as its "intangible" powers or "soft assets"—productive, market, sales, and human development factors. This combination of hard and soft assets must be recognized, built, diffused, and networked. Among other factors, this combination of hard and soft assets includes a company's

- Brand names investment, together with the quality and the customer satisfaction it delivers on those brands
- Technology and know-how and the patent rights that institutionalize some of this
- Customer relationships and distribution arrangements
- Partnerships with suppliers and other business alliances
- International and global connections
- Capacity to attract and retain capable people, together with human resources and other training and development skills
- International and global connections
- Content of public responsibility orientation and environmental responsiveness
- Effectiveness of processes and integration of technological, management, and human resources factors
- Perceived quality value of products and services
- Responsibility of corporate governance

This business principle is far from new except in terms of the new emphasis by pacesetter companies on its actual *execution* rather than just viewing it as a generalized *philosophy*. It has come into fundamental economic focus in the quiet (but nonetheless powerful) development that has been taking place in the way investment in companies has been changing. A principal difference has been these companies' understanding—and their effectiveness in the management—of the tectonic shift in the twenty-first century's character of business value-added creation and its impact on driving strong business results and competitiveness. This has fundamentally changed the meaning and content of business financial capital and thus the meaning and power of management capital for accelerating and sustaining business profitability and growth.

In technical, economic (i.e., Federal Reserve Board) terms (as shown in Figure 2), 50 years ago tangible "hard" assets—brick and mortar, equipment, and inventories—represented 78 percent of the assets of U.S. nonfinancial corporations. Today that proportion is down to 53 percent—an enormous reduction—as a result of growth in the impact of brands, technology, customer and supplier relations, quality, and other intangible assets in powering business growth. What has driven this is in terms of economic estimates (according to the Federal Reserve Bank of Philadelphia) is the fact that annual investment in intangible "soft" assets—research and development, advertising, software purchases, and so on—rose from 4 percent of gross domestic product in 1978 to almost 10 percent in 2000, an enormous two and one-half times increase.

The twenty-first-century management model that characterizes today's corporate winning ways is built in terms of leadership and management understanding of and focus on the value-added intangibles and soft assets fully as much as the hard assets, and in some markets far more. It changes the meaning, skills, tools, and emphasis of management. It greatly accelerates corporate business results and sustains them as fixed stars in the business horizon rather than as the comets and fireworks displays of some corporate operations that have died and been buried without an autopsy.

One of the primary characteristics of this new management model is its meaning and emphasis in regard to innovation. This is characterized by the institutionalization of—and the infrastructure and integration for—constant *management* innovation, especially of these all-powerful intangibles. This also has become a necessary condition for successful product research and development (R&D). The reason for this development is that today the most significant characteristic of a successful business innovation is that it also positions a company for the next innovation—it is not just an end in itself. The not-very-successful approach

Figure 2 Ratio of Market Cap to Book Value (after data: Federal Reserve, in *Wall Street Journal,* April 4, 2002)

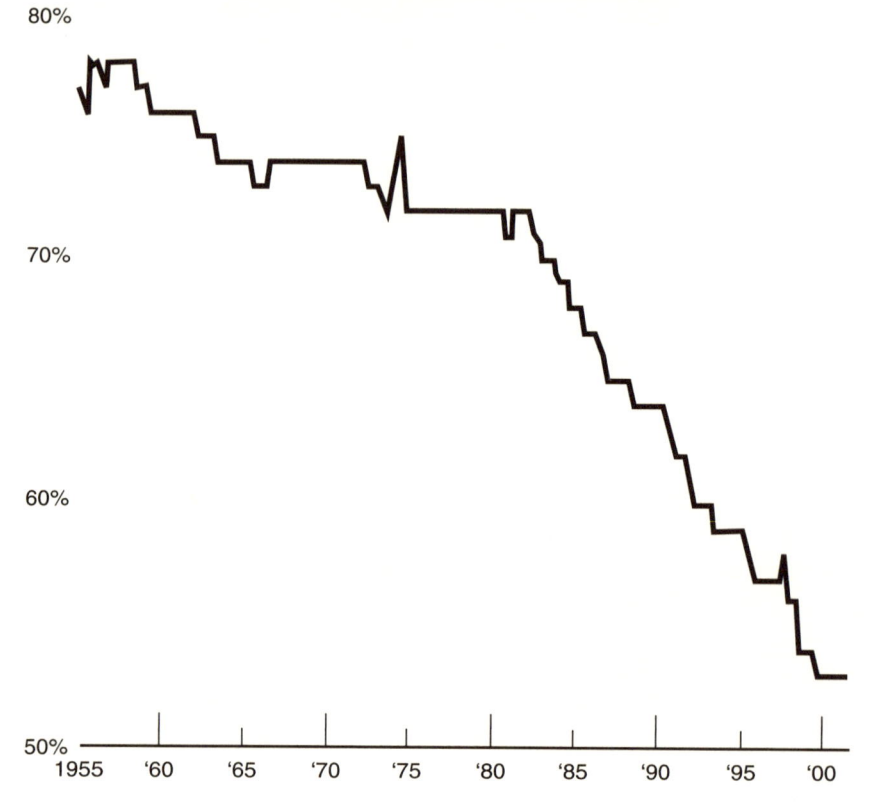

Tangible Assets as a Percent of All Assets of Nonfinancial Businesses

to this in the twentieth century was through the old, now-long-downsized corporate staffs, which are not missed because they were operating within the traditional management model that the change in the tectonic plates of the modern economy has made increasingly shaky and undependable.

OPERATIONALIZING THE NEW CONCEPTS OF THE TWENTY-FIRST-CENTURY COMPANY

The thing that sets pacesetter companies apart is their effectiveness in the third fundamental change in management. Pacesetter companies have systematically *operationalized* this concept of the twenty-first-century company, just as they have systematically converted technology concepts into successful products and services. They have taken this from an abstract idea (i.e., something merely presented at executive platforms or seminar discussions) to a strong results-focused competitive strength, with emphasis on management innovation in its many new and broader forms. As was discussed earlier, operationalizing emphasizes measuring these results on a case-by-case, hands-on basis, which also can contribute to the progressive quantification of *intangible* factors in terms that can then begin to be combined with the existing quantification of *tangible* factors.

For example, among the very early pacesetting companies was General Electric, which developed its "boundaryless" behavior initiative for focusing the entire company on breaking down the walls of traditional decentralization, which was the heart of the hierarchical concept of the corporation. Another leading-edge example of such innovation is Wal-Mart's management emphasis on integrating the best of traditional merchandising and supplier practices with the best of the new information and other technology initiatives. Wal-Mart is constantly moving in the direction of not allowing those initiatives to act as separate silos on the company's operating horizon. This has blindsided much of the consumer merchandising industry and continues to do so.

On the merchandising side has been Wal-Mart's emphasis on face-to-face, multichannel selling of broad ranges of goods, from shoes to furniture, and of services, from optical products to pharmaceuticals. On the technology side is the integrated support given to this through the widely based Internet supply chain network that connects with resources ranging from shoes to financial services. Reportedly, links to banks may enable suppliers to be paid as soon as a purchase crosses the bar-code reader at checkout. This greatly accelerates the immediacy of the suppliers' cash flow, and this prompt payment also allows Wal-Mart to demand discounts from suppliers that can translate into lower prices. Everyone wins—except Wal-Mart's competitors.

Examples also abound throughout the communications, computer, software, server, and Internet industries. One of the original leaders was Dell Computer in markets where competition was initially based on *product* leadership, but then the products increasingly were commoditized. Because Dell emphasized its business *management innovation* of direct-to-buyer sales discipline through its marketing effectiveness processes (originally by telecommunications and then over the Internet), it was able to leap forward in its markets by making an end run around its more traditional distribution-focused competitors.

Many other companies are emphasizing the aggressive implementation of major management innovation breakthroughs, which they are achieving by systematically benchmarking other companies. For example, a study was conducted by professors at the Georgia Institute of Technology and the College of William and Mary. That study evaluated more than 600 companies with strong total quality management initiatives (which were positively confirmed by rigorous award criteria practices). The results of the study showed the major performance differences, over a five-year period, between companies that emphasized best practices and benchmarking and control group companies. As is shown in Figure 3, the companies that emphasized best practices and benchmarking averaged a 44 percent higher stock price return, a 48 percent higher growth in operating income, and a 37 percent higher growth in sales.

CAPITALIZING MANAGEMENT POWER: THE OVERARCHING THEME
Although these examples of management innovation illustrate significant business results, they nonetheless reflect only the early stages of the emphasis on management capital. When management capital is properly understood, structured, led throughout a company, and relentlessly emphasized, it is the key to accelerating and sustaining profitable business results.

This leads to the fourth area of fundamental change in the management content and practices of pacesetter companies. These companies emphasize the principle that business management innovation is not an *event* but is instead an overarching and constant management and leadership attitude, theme, and *process*. This attitude and process defines the organization and initiatives for its implementation—not the other way around, as in the old hierarchy of the traditional company that focused only on its hard assets. Even Disney—a company that epitomizes promotional phenomena—must innovate regularly because of the rapid changes in the expectations of its consumer buyers.

Our attempts to help our customer companies sustain growth has demonstrated what is at the root of the success of pacesetter businesses in this brutally competitive economy. The root of success in sustaining growth is an increasing yet clearly evolving emphasis on developing the strategy for and implementation of a clear business focus on "capitalizing" these new powers for the breadth of business leadership.

In our work we have termed this a company's *management capital*. It is the business's overarching theme for capitalizing the management power for recognizing, developing, accumulating, deploying, and measuring the capacity and effectiveness of the company's total resources to

Figure 3 Management of Quality Innovation Results (after Vinod Singh, associate professor, Georgia Institute of Technology and Kevin Hendricks, associate professor, College of William and Mary)

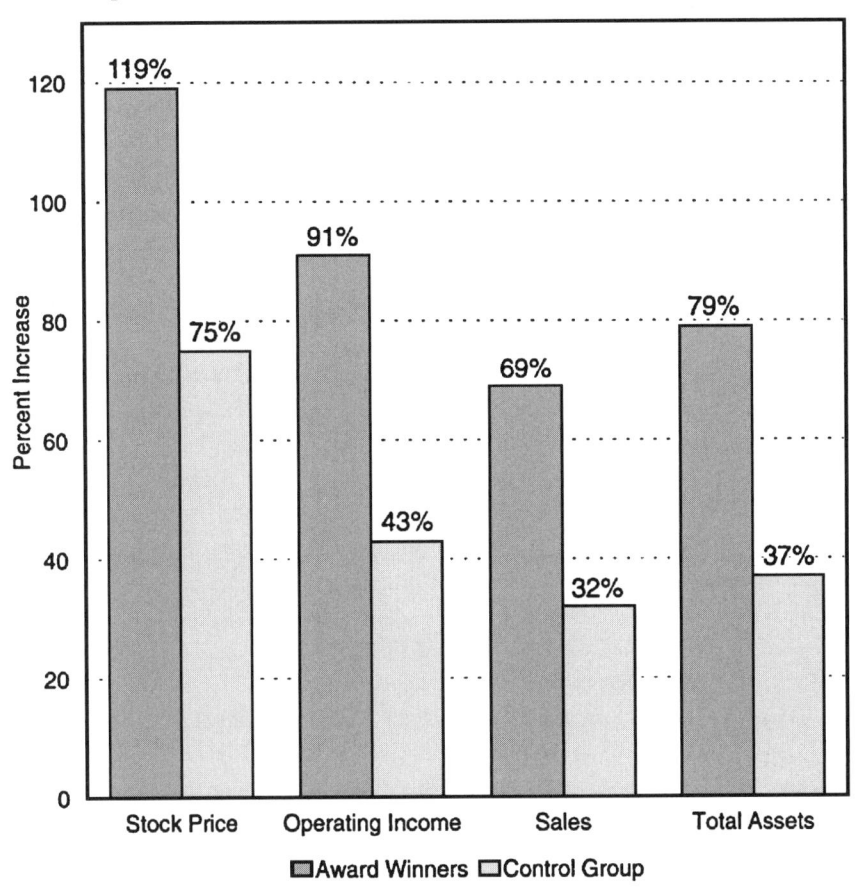

Category	Award Winners	Control Group
Stock Price	119%	75%
Operating Income	91%	43%
Sales	69%	32%
Total Assets	79%	37%

Source: Georgia Institute of Technology

sustain and accelerate its business growth and profitability. These resources include the company's "soft" as well as "hard" assets, and the focus on the company's total resources is to implement business innovation so that the company can relentlessly increase its product, service, and other business value for customers and key stakeholders. Management capital focuses on converging the opportunistic growth strength once thought of as "New Economy" with the fiscal responsibility of "Old Economy" discipline.

Attention to this management power emphasizes identifying and overcoming the backward creep and the disconnects that can have been obscured by a strong business period or by outmoded standards. It emphasizes energizing the business network culture, whose defining characteristic is the speed of successful results. Its environment is one of open communications that develop the creativity of individual job entrepreneurs throughout the organization.

This is a critically important fundamental dimension of the evolution of the continuously strong performance of long-term business powerhouses as diverse as General Electric, Intel, and Union Pacific, as well as many other strong and growing twenty-first-century businesses. The successful confluence of this kind of management with technology is the similar source of strength of businesses ranging from Dell to Wal-Mart. It is also the key to the ongoing prospects of e-businesses such as E-Bay and Amazon. And it has been the basis for the resurgence of great technology-driven corporations such as Nokia and IBM.

Its value emphasis is led and managed as a basic strategy for competitiveness, with hands-on leadership very different from those management models in which customer and other value emphasis was seen and managed in terms of a technical operational emphasis and strong standards and practices. As important as these areas remain, the new model adds an emphasis on continuous strategic alignment of product and service value with the upward-moving value expectations of customers.

This is fundamental to the effective establishment and implementation of business value-added measurements, which provide overview indicators of how well a company is using its economic capital assets. These business value-added measurements are among the ultimate determinants of the market-to-book ratios of today's companies in the face of the many other important measurements that are employed, such as market position (whether a company is number one or number two or just an also-ran), patent life, and other measurements.

In management capital terms, there are three fundamental factors in regard to the ways these value-added measures are implemented and used:

1. They provide total measures of the company's business results.
2. They make the meaning of "operational value" explicit in the company instead of its being a mere promotional statement in executive speeches.
3. They make these measures widely available as part of organization-wide learning.

The communications goal is to help every person in the company think more and more about the company's performance (in financial terms as well as in terms of its products and services), as its investors and customers do.

Management capital's crucial importance to business success—in various terms and in several terminologies—has in practical fact long been an extremely important informed judgment consideration that is widely recognized in principle throughout the business investment community and in businesses.

Supply chain managers and purchasing agents have long recognized management capital as an important factor in their buying decisions, especially in terms of a company's reliability as a long-term supplier. In addition, savvy employees have always had an instinctive consideration of management capital when they size up organizations to decide where they can have the best jobs. And corporate managers have long relied on their assessment of a company's management capital when determining their expectations for generating strong organizational performance.

IMPLEMENTING MANAGEMENT CAPITAL AS A LEADING INDICATOR FOR SUSTAINING PROFITABILITY AND GROWTH

The implementation of this management capital capacity, as will be discussed in later chapters, involves the following factors:

- The leadership and management passion, populism, and disciplined responsibility that bring focus to the theme, underpin the processes for its continuous implementation, and develop the character of the company.
- The creation and continuing development of the environment and framework for involving the creativity, knowledge, skills, and attitudes of everyone in the organization in all components of the process of developing improved results.
- The systematic identification of the major business issues and opportunities confronting top-line growth and bottom-line profitability in the company in terms of value creation for customers, investors, and employees. This has to do with "visible" issues, as will be discussed later in this book—issues related to product, service, and market—and "invisible" issues—related to the way the company accomplishes this, with measurement of related business failure

costs. The relentless and rigorous development and improvement of the strategy, discipline, and process in the key management channels in ways that both solve current problems and create new business opportunities.
- The digitizing of key business operations and processes as economically appropriate, and, above all, the effective ongoing emphasis on effective execution of all these initiatives to promote competitive leadership.

The result of all this is that management capital effectiveness (and the systems and process leadership that underpin it) is explicitly becoming one of the powerful new central leading indicators of sustained corporate profitability and growth in the twenty-first-century economy. Management capital is one of the key factors by which corporate growth and earnings can be predicted, and it is an important component of economic analysis in dealing with some of the issues discussed at the beginning of this chapter. Moreover, it is a major factor in the focus and meaning of managing with an attitude that will sustain growth in the period of new economic challenges now facing companies.

Our experience shows that accomplishing this is very much driven by a company's leadership and management attitudes that reflect the new economic, human, technological, and global demands for sustaining profitable business growth. The attitudes—not a new bureaucracy rising on the corporate horizon—create this new management model and its organization and implementation. Implementation will, of course, continue to vary among companies, depending on markets, product and service content, personalities, competitive conditions, and other circumstances.

CHAPTER 3

EMPHASIZING QUALITY OF MANAGEMENT INSTEAD OF QUANTITY OF MANAGEMENT

IN THE HIGHLY DEMANDING BEGINNING YEARS of the twenty-first century many companies and business leaders have a *quality of management* that is a new competitive leadership combination of *passion, populism,* and *disciplined responsibility.* This quality of management has become a common denominator even though these companies and leaders may differ in their history, personality, evolution, and markets. It also is the basic foundation for capitalizing the management power that was discussed in Chapter 2.

QUALITY—NOT QUANTITY—OF MANAGEMENT

Today's pacesetter companies do not view their strength in enabling growth in terms of the *quantity of management* of the hierarchical leadership of an earlier day. Instead, they emphasize the *quality of management,* which recognizes and is measured in terms of leadership and networking capability for focusing a company's total resources on sustaining business growth.

They implement these results through effectiveness in developing and deploying management capital's intellectual, technical, human information, and other resources in integrating a company's "hard" and "soft" assets. This takes place through the processes, tools, and strategies that help each man and woman in the company think, learn, act, and make decisions about how he or she both individually and as part of a team can help provide the superior value for customers and, consequently, for investors that meets today's accelerating business demands.

The objective is not to increase the emphasis on additional managerial techniques nor to establish a few more high-level management departments on the company's organization chart nor to create a new systems bureaucracy. Instead, the objective is to create constant momentum for establishing and maintaining competitive leadership in *all*— not just some, as in traditional Old-Economy companies—the principal management channels across the company's business value chain. These channels include product development, supply management, operations effectiveness, and quality, as well as others, all of which will be discussed more fully later in this chapter. The ultimate goal is to deploy and integrate the company's full capabilities. These principal management channels facilitate a company's leadership effectiveness so that the company can better use not only its financial and physical assets but particularly its human, technical, intellectual, and informational resources for better planning; better care of the company's customers; and better creating, selling, and delivering of the products and services for those customers.

Essentially, this quality-of-management leadership emphasis develops, implements, and maintains systematic capabilities that establish, align, and integrate a company's strategy, objectives, goals, and measurements with its work, teamwork processes, and execution tools. It does this in all the company's key business areas. It is the foundation of an organization's balanced—not piecemeal—approach to leadership, and it prioritizes a company's actions throughout the full scope of its improvement opportunities and requirements. It is fully integrated with the company's drivers of sales-revenue.

The key point is this: It is the attitude, process, and management capital disciplines that create the structure and organization for this quality-of management emphasis—not vice versa. Furthermore, the management capital structure may vary among companies because it is determined by each company's history, markets, personality, and requirements.

LEADERSHIP ACTIONS SUSTAIN COMPANY GROWTH

After all, management knowledge has become globalized. For example, consider the following new best practices in management:

- The Internet
- Short-cycle delivery
- Use of customer-led client servers
- Building to customer order instead of to stock
- Process management
- Total quality leadership
- The logistics of outsourcing
- First-or-second-or-out market leadership strategy
- Lean team management.

All these practices exist today in many companies and many industries. This knowledge is discussed in the same terms but in different languages around the world: in Chicago, Santa Clara, Mexico City, Buenos Aires, São Paulo, Detroit, Atlanta, Houston, Shanghai, Singapore, Tokyo, Dusseldorf, and Paris.

However, there is an enormous difference in the business results among companies. Indeed, some companies may be two or three times more effective in their implementation of this management knowledge to achieve successful results. Inscriptions on university buildings state that knowledge is power. However, business experience shows that this is true only when there are leaders who understand that a company's *culture* for sustaining growth is defined primarily by its *actions* for growth and for systematically identifying and removing the *roadblocks* to growth while it is also installing new drivers. The quality of leadership and management passion, populism, and disciplined responsibility is crucial to the effectiveness of the management capital discipline found in pacesetter companies. This quality must be pervasive throughout the systematic analysis, planning, and construction components of the management capital discipline in order to achieve the desired business results.

The next three sections of this chapter discuss each component of this new leadership and management quality: passion, populism, and disciplined responsibility.

THE LEADERSHIP AND MANAGEMENT QUALITY OF *PASSION*

Passion is found in leadership that recognizes that the pursuit of excellence is the most powerful emotional motivator in any organization. In addition, passionate leaders have a bias for action in implementing this ethic throughout the organization.

This ethic and this approach define the basic competitive values of an organization. For example, "human resources" means the development of individual opportunity and responsibility as well as team actions instead of the traditional definition pertaining to employee benefit plans and training programs. Similarly, goals are to be met; they are not just "best efforts." E-business and the Internet mean a business model and a way of managing, not just the application of technology. Planning means being fact-based. There is always a "plan B." What one measures correctly one can accomplish correctly. Innovation and imagination are encouraged, and careers are not penalized if the risks taken do not always succeed. Implementation is the basic common denominator, and the concrete business results are the indicator of the organization's performance.

Passionate leadership also recognizes that a company's business performance changes and improves only when the behavior of managers and employees changes and improves in terms of its leadership with respect to customers, markets, and profitability. Passionate leaders understand that the organization's culture for improvement is the collective result of the organization's actions and can be affected only by the constant hands-on improvement of those actions; in other words, passionate leaders do not delay in taking action and do not waste time simply making speeches that create fireworks displays instead of process improvements.

Passionate leadership has a sureness and lightness of touch that recognizes that good management and the management capital that implements it work best when one scarcely knows that they are there. It gives reality to a modernized version of the traditional Oriental principle that goes something like this:

> A weak leader is someone from whom employees turn away.
>
> A strong leader is someone whom employees turn toward.
>
> A great leader is someone about whom employees say, "We did it ourselves."

THE LEADERSHIP AND MANAGEMENT QUALITY OF *POPULISM*

The *populism* aspect of this leadership and management quality emphasizes throughout the company's workplaces what the failed management practices of the past overlooked or even purged: the fundamental competitive business strength that comes from fully utilizing the organizationwide knowledge, skills, and attitudes about the freedom to innovate, about solving problems cooperatively, and about the value of teamwork that the great majority of the people who work already bring to their jobs because of the basic traditions of democratic life. Its hallmark is to return the fizz—the enthusiasm—to working in the organization, in contrast to the apathetic environment that continues to dominate in some companies.

Populist leadership is demonstrated by a deep confidence in the capabilities of people throughout the company to bring about these improvements *when employees are provided with the organization, flexibility, and appropriate support to make improvements*. Populist leaders understand that this is a key to the management capital attitude and is essential in providing the foundation for profitable business growth.

Populist leadership creates openness, trust, and communication throughout the company (and up and down the hierarchy) in order to establish an environment for what might be thought of as *individual improvement entrepreneurship* in the company. In other words, it encourages people to develop their own forms of teamwork and their personal ownership of competitive improvement. There is always a better way, and the people who are closest to the work and operations are the ones who are most likely to discover and implement that better way. Any improvement in work and jobs throughout an organization—even if it's only a small percentage improvement—compounds at a remarkable rate, and it can create a competitive leadership difference.

THE LEADERSHIP AND MANAGEMENT QUALITY OF *DISCIPLINED RESPONSIBILITY*

The *disciplined responsibility* aspect of this leadership and management quality occurs when managers recognize that no improvement can be made unless there is a relentless emphasis on creating, measuring, maintaining, and systematically structuring a company's focus on its financial, intellectual, human, informational, technological, and other tangible and intangible capacities and resource strengths. Discipline provides the basis for constantly accelerating value for customers, investors, employees, the environment, and the public. Disciplined leadership emphasizes the development of the *totality* of the company's resources, and it is supported by the management capital attitude for sustaining sound business growth and continuously creating the management innovations that help drive and escalate that growth.

Disciplined responsibility is essential to the character, positioning, and overview of corporate governance. Taken together, these factors equate to leadership whose *disciplined responsibility* develops and structures the foundation of the *passion* and *populism* to create value for customers and other stakeholders. A fundamental dimension of this disciplined responsibility lies in focusing on the importance of implementing, maintaining, and emphasizing the systematic capabilities that establish, align, balance, and integrate a company's strategies, objectives, goals, and measurements throughout its management capital channels and its work and teamwork processes. Disciplined responsibility is the foundation of the leadership that establishes an organization's balanced, integrated, and prioritized actions throughout the full scope of its business opportunities and requirements. It emphasizes the passion and populism for assuring the organization's value-creation capability through the following strengths:

- Companywide understanding of the company's vision and the management and leadership values for achieving sustained growth
- Clearly defined goals, including both measured business financial value-added and measured business quality value-added expectations

- Strategies in whose development people throughout the entire organization can play a major role and that are discussed and communicated as broadly as possible to develop organizationwide learning
- The planning of integration on a companywide basis, with focused objectives that are directly connected with the strategies
- Full alignment of these operating plans and measurements with the company's business, financial, and quality goals
- Effective relationship of measurements—financial, operating, and others—to each other and to the company's strategies and plans
- Criteria and mechanisms for performance management in line with plans, together with alignment with the "plan B"s to allow an effective approach to surprises and unexpected situations
- Emphasis on timely integration of joint ventures, mergers, divestitures, and acquisitions with operating and business plans and performance management
- Systematic asset management—including financial capital allocation and asset portfolio structuring—in accordance with financial business and operating plans
- Proactive management "handles" for leading operations through basic performance indicators, specialized plans, and clear action mechanisms
- Development steps for recruiting, evaluating, training, and encouraging the development of the people who are the keys to the company's growth
- Specifically defined actions to identify and eliminate the business disconnects that stand in the way of achieving these results, as well as increasingly improved measurement of the return-on-investment performance of the company's management capital, in terms of sales revenue, capacity enhancement, and cost reduction.
- The foundation for continually "morphing," that is, developing and transforming the effectiveness of the company's management approach with management leadership and innovation, and positioning the company for the business demands of the twenty-first century throughout the key management capital channels through which the business' results are driven and sustained

PRINCIPAL MANAGEMENT CAPITAL CHANNELS

Business experience has identified 12 key channels of management capital in pacesetter companies:

1. New product/service development and introduction for product leadership through more rapid and economical development and introduction of successful new products and services
2. Marketing effectiveness for market leadership and top-line growth, through effective market development and customer relationship management
3. Business expansion and globalization for creating value by leveraging resources and capabilities across international business boundaries
4. Total quality for product, process, and service excellence to assure complete customer satisfaction, profitability, and top-line growth
5. Management measurement for managing performance and improvement via key operating measurements
6. Partnership and alliance development for competitive leadership through the effective development of production and strategically effective business relationships
7. Operations effectiveness for operating cost leadership, performance excellence, and integrated management of operating activities
8. Supply management for effective management of all supply relationships to increase effectiveness and reduce costs and delivery cycle time
9. Human resources effectiveness for encouraging the integration of the individual knowledge, skills and attitudes development, commitment, and effectiveness of all personnel
10. Integrated business information management for improved availability and integrity of the information required to manage the business
11. Financial operations effectiveness for leadership in financial operations to support and assure growth, profitability, and complete customer satisfaction
12. Asset management for managing the effective acquisition, utilization, and disposition of necessary assets and infrastructure

A company's effectiveness in these key channels—and their coincidence with the company's opportunity areas—is a key to its competitive strength. This effectiveness goes far beyond the application of information technology, which is of course critically important. These management channels provide the platforms for delivering leading-edge technology results, which otherwise are too often delayed, reduced, or not realized at all because of disconnects with the business operations.

Effectiveness is generated in these channels by means of competitive leadership in the systems and end-to-end processes, tools, resources, and strategies that create the basic learning framework and motivational strength. This helps and encourages each person in the organization, both individually and in teams, to think, act, and make decisions about how to provide superior performance. The effectiveness generated in these channels is also the means by which the company's leadership implements actions for serving the company's customers, investors, and employees by delivering consistently improved and fully responsible business value and has the measurements to indicate that it is in fact doing so.

AN EXAMPLE: CREATING MOMENTUM TO SUSTAIN GROWTH IN THE GLOBAL BUSINESS VALUE CHAIN

For example, a large international manufacturing and services company has been widely broadening its global presence in the last decade through a series of acquisitions and joint ventures around the world. The company has been very profitable—in fact, it is the unquestioned global leader in several markets—and historically had been competitively dominant in the development and installation of competitive leadership processes throughout those markets.

However, the company's new leadership recognized key problem areas throughout the company's global value chain in continuing to implement its growth strategy in its served markets under new competitive international demands. It focused on a new, more aggressive innovative momentum through a new quality of management with the passion, populism, and disciplined responsibility to sustain and accelerate the company's growth.

Recognizing the limitations in the company's existing emphasis on capitalizing its strength to support this growth, the company's leaders determined that the following areas required significant focus and improvement:

- The company had continued to evolve throughout its several acquisitions and alliances as a collection of operations that were not managed as truly integrated global businesses. The growing size of the businesses had become a *weakness*, not a strength.
- Global business plans had not been systematically integrated; instead, they were bundled together. Consequently, they did not always take advantage of the full range of growth opportunities provided by the company's full integration.
- Business opportunities were defined too narrowly: The business framework was more for routine actions than for opportunistic entrepreneurship.
- The "horizontal" and local creation of value in this chain was not well understood or effectively leveraged. This local business was often thought of as "untidy" by the corporate parent compared with its traditional vertical operations.
- Improvements were approached incrementally. The objectives of several business segments were simply to be "better than last year" because that had been their original success formula, in contrast to relentless breakthrough leadership.
- Organizationwide, different departments did not work together effectively; consequently, there were unbalanced activities, and this led to a frequent emphasis on "strong controls."
- Internet and e-business initiatives had been slow and had not produced the intended results both because of infrastructure issues and because of e-frastructure disconnects.
- Some key business segments continued to carry the company business results, while the intended growth of others continued to fail to meet expectations.
- There was little capability for knowledge diffusion throughout the organization to assure that what worked well in some company segments became quickly available in all the segments to which it was applicable.
- Actions were too often implemented without relentless development of the necessary people-based improvement, knowledge, attitudes, rewards, and skills.
- Cost management had become an oxymoron in some significant areas. In spite of accounting processes, managers did not always know what things really cost.

- Customer value acceleration had been greatly limited because of the need to pull products through a group of individual corporate units.
- Resource planning, including technology and human resources, had not been clearly structured.

THE POWER OF FACT-BASED QUALITY OF MANAGEMENT

This company performed a detailed analysis of its 12 principal management capital channels in order to evaluate the effectiveness of specific work and teamwork components of the company's resources—that is, in terms of its customers, markets, technology, information resources, human resources, and brand and intellectual resources. The company determined that the aggregate effectiveness throughout those channels was 35 to 40 percent for meeting the demands for sustaining the company's strong strategic growth. Moreover, there was very limited business integration among these resources and the management channels that focused them, and there was very poor alignment with the company's market and customer strategy.

Nonetheless, some of the existing company segments emphasized to the new management the business and market successes that had been achieved through those channels and served as a caution against arguing with success and rocking some successful business boats. The company's new leadership, as a precondition to beginning the evaluation, therefore had wisely established the fact-based emphasis of the work, which made possible reasoned discussions on the areas in question and recognition and acceptance of the requirements for improvement actions.

For example, consider the marketing effectiveness channel: Whereas in some U.S. markets there were some very strong growth areas, sales and account growth throughout many other American markets ranged from only slight increases to flat to strongly negative trends in account retention and customer growth. The cause throughout several of those markets was strong and progressive disconnects from the increasing expectations of the company's customers. However, the great hazard to sustaining the company's growth that this represented had not stood out clearly because of increases in the company's top-line sales growth caused by some price increases and the few major growth areas. Additionally, the company was starting to lose market share to new competitors that had been entering these markets.

Moreover, the high and growing costs of customer service and customer complaints had been justified as necessary for supporting good customer relationships. However, data showed that sometimes more than 40 percent of the customers whose service needs had been satisfied nonetheless did not buy again from the company.

Additionally, these customer relationships were not adequately aided or supported through suitable integration and full use of company capabilities in the information management channel. The company was not fully using its information technology and Internet strengths for detailed customer information collection, analysis, and reporting.

Furthermore, in human resource channel terms, training was not adequate for the utilization of this information when it became available. This problem was worsened by human relations motivation issues in which employee dissatisfaction resulting from supervisory, promotional, and economic disconnects correlated with customer dissatisfaction.

Aggressive support of these strong top-line, as well as bottom-line, growth objectives required far better integration with the development both of product offerings in the new product development channel and of service processes and much more powerful use of the company's strong brand names.

MOMENTUM FOR MAJOR MANAGEMENT BUSINESS INNOVATION RESULTS

As the company's leaders planned the necessary management business innovations to solve these problems, and as the company began to implement the corresponding new and improved delivery systems and processes, significant momentum for new business results began. For example, the marketing effectiveness channel began improvement of its focus on customers through two changes: first, new emphasis on information management as well as human resources and training to increase understanding of customer needs, and second, strong adjustments and changes in both product offerings and service processes. The information management human resource and training emphasis and product and service changes allowed better application of resources and provided significant new growth in both new customer accounts and account retention.

This customer account growth generated a new upsurge in sales revenue and market share, a significant reduction in customer dissatisfaction, and a major reduction in costs. Figure 4 shows the resulting major growth in customer accounts, which has become a major driver in meeting the company's strategic objective of sustaining strong growth in sales and earnings.

Figure 5 shows how this company significantly clarified its management responsibilities and relationships. The company successfully integrated actions both within and among several of its management channels, particularly those pertaining to marketing effectiveness, information management, human resources, and new product development, as well as other

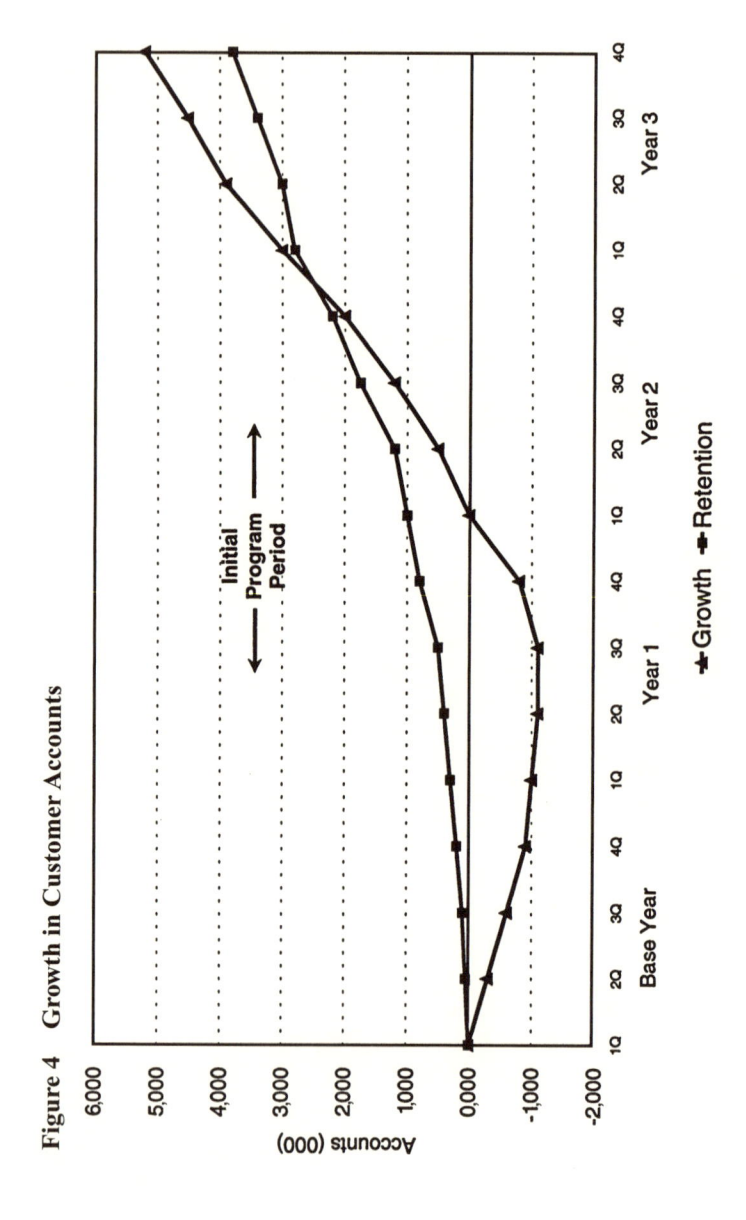

Figure 4 Growth in Customer Accounts

CHAPTER 3   EMPHASIZING QUALITY OF MANAGEMENT

management channels. That successful integration had a very powerful ongoing effect on the company's accumulation of its management capital strength and the consequent impact on business results.

Figure 6 shows the total business results of the company's quality-of-management emphasis on management capital discipline in terms of large reductions in costs as well as growth of income. The company leadership has continued to focus on management capital accumulation to assure the continuous development of its management process innovation as a fundamental factor in its constant drive to sustain its growth in sales and earnings.

EXORCISING 10 WORN-OUT MANAGEMENT DOCTRINES

This example and many others like it reflect the emphasis on this quality-of-management approach and its management capital power. It recognizes the essential demand for creating new business momentum and growth for explicitly identifying and exorcising the worn-out business and management doctrines that are irrelevant and ineffective in today's tough economic environment and that are carryovers from the quantity-of-management days. Although they are increasingly being purged by today's pacesetters, these worn-out doctrines are still driving values in some companies.

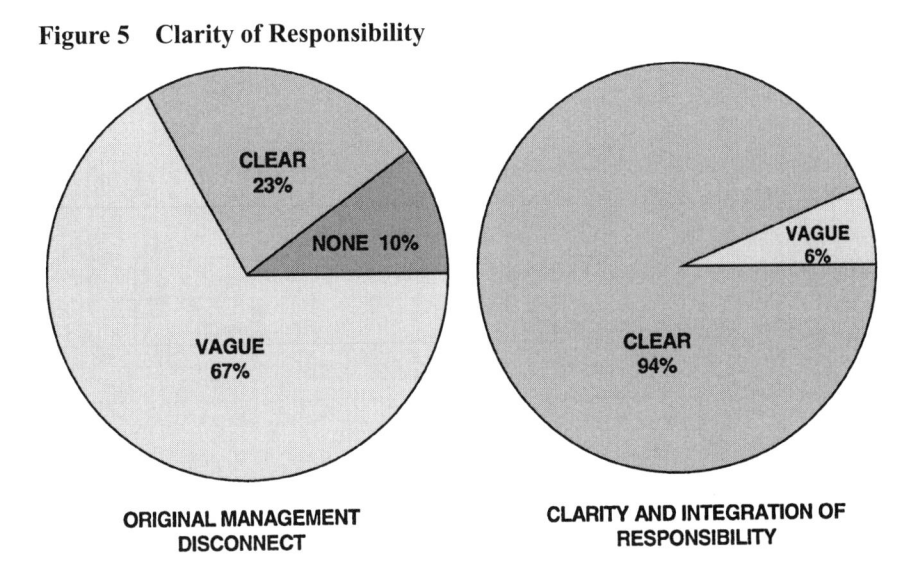

Figure 5   Clarity of Responsibility

ORIGINAL MANAGEMENT DISCONNECT	CLARITY AND INTEGRATION OF RESPONSIBILITY
CLEAR 23% / NONE 10% / VAGUE 67%	CLEAR 94% / VAGUE 6%

50 THE POWER OF MANAGEMENT CAPITAL

Figure 6   Company Business Results

ADDITIONAL SALES REVENUE – CUMULATIVE IMPROVEMENT

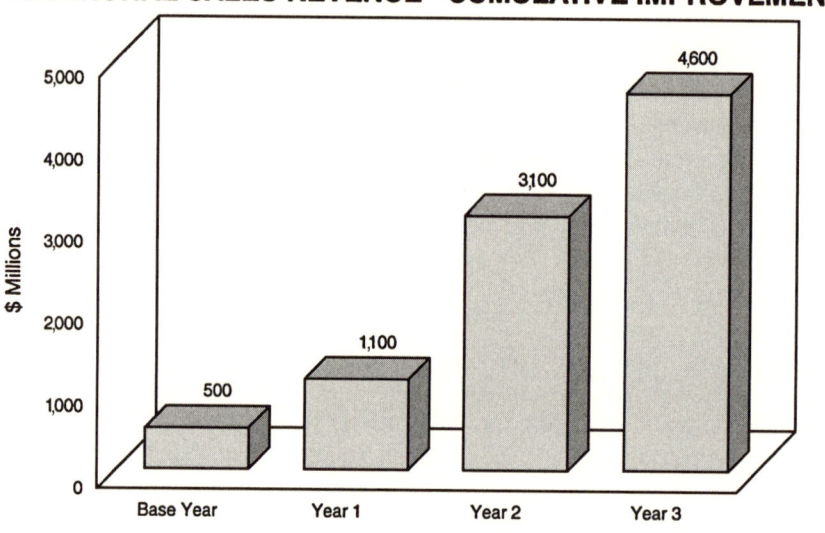

Period	$ Millions
Base Year	500
Year 1	1,100
Year 2	3,100
Year 3	4,600

REDUCED OPERATING COSTS – CUMULATIVE SAVINGS

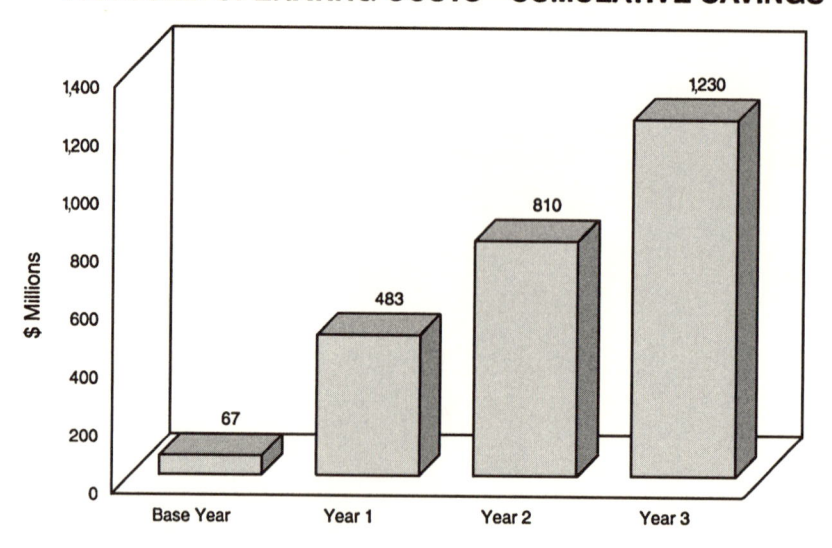

Period	$ Millions
Base Year	67
Year 1	483
Year 2	810
Year 3	1,230

The following sections describe 10 of these worn-out management doctrines that are no longer helpful in today's economy.

WORN-OUT DOCTRINE 1: Good Management Means Getting the Ideas out of the Boss's Head and into the Hands of the Workers

Today we know that it is far more than that. Good management means empowering the knowledge, skills, learning process, and attitudes of everyone in the organization with work and teamwork improvement processes that each person understands, believes in, and helps implement. It means getting everyone to understand that recognition and reward in the organization no longer depend solely on making the boss happy, because what an employee does to make the *customer* happy will also make a smart boss happy.

WORN-OUT DOCTRINE 2: Corporate and Management Change Must Be Incremental

Today we know that to be effective, company improvement can also be approached on a broad front, with full attention to the development of organizationwide human understanding and support. Trying to cut off the cat's tail an inch at a time creates a bias for delay that can cause a company to wait out change much too long and create human and customer conflict, as many companies have found in the postmortem of their recent experiences. The key is skill in establishing the sequence of improvement *prioritization* so that one does not have to do *everything* before one does anything. It is like playing rotation pool, where skills mean you always have the double objective of both pocketing the ball and positioning yourself for your next shot.

WORN-OUT DOCTRINE 3: The Primary Way to Succeed Is to Make Products or Offer Services Quicker and Cheaper, Sell Them Hard, Finance Them Cleverly, and Provide a Service Safety Net for Customers When Unsatisfactory Products Come Through

This totally misses the enormous changes in customer expectations for value and for essentially perfect products and the enormous price in lost customers and product repair that this creates. Today's competitive leaders operate in terms of the far different doctrine that the best way to make products and offer services quicker and cheaper is to make and sell them better.

WORN-OUT DOCTRINE 4: The Internet Is Primarily a Technology

The Internet is much more than technology; it is a *business model* with processes that can anticipate customer behaviors, recognize market changes, cultivate new skills for managers and employees, and provide the potential for significant sales additions to revenues. Today's pacesetter companies approach the Internet as though it were an ecosystem in which a company is connected both externally with suppliers and customers and internally as a network among employees.

WORN-OUT DOCTRINE 5: Emphasis on Traditional Cost Accounting Is the Primary Basis for Reducing Costs and Focusing Business Improvement

This emphasis can sometimes miss key opportunities and embedded unneeded costs. After many years of cost accounting, some companies still do not know what their real costs are.

One of the reasons for this is that the processes that precede and follow the physical creation of products and services sometimes have not been the focus of traditional cost measurement but today represent a significant proportion of the opportunity for improvement. Today we know that these real opportunities for improvement are best focused by cost measurement approaches that are integrated with these physical process activities and are reflected in process-oriented measurements such as quality cost, material flow, and logistics costs, which also identify failure costs that should be targeted for improvement.

WORN-OUT DOCTRINE 6: A Single-Dimensioned Emphasis on an Internally Focused Approach to Improvement Generates the Earliest and Best Results

However, experience shows that this approach can sometimes *divert* company attention away from customer and employee development and motivation and *distract* emphasis from identifying and building on the organization's fundamental strengths for understanding and serving customers. In some organizations this internal focus has generated the organizational churning for some of the specialists and middle managers—on whom much of the company's operational strength depends—that has created the day-by-day uncertainty that they did not know when they woke up in the morning whether they would have a job. Today we know that a multidimensional integrated management foundation is an essential framework for realistic improvement. One can never unscramble broken organization eggs by reassembling the white, the yolk, and the albumen that have been spilled because of the dissipation of the organization's strength for connecting with and serving its customers through an unduly heavy-handed emphasis on improvement.

WORN-OUT DOCTRINE 7: Organization Decentralization Is Invariably a Good Approach as an End in Itself

Today we know that decentralization must be carefully balanced and evaluated; otherwise, huge long-term problems ensue, for example, in the following areas:

- The allocation of financial capital—because the larger units can have the clout even though the smaller units might have the future.
- Marketing—because of lack of interest in cross selling or regarding distribution in the speed and economy of full loads and common carriers.
- Operating cost leadership—because of the desire to hold on to business activities that could far better be outsourced.

Today we know that it is competitively essential to use company size as a strength—not a weakness—through suitable integration of common resources that benefit all business units.

WORN-OUT DOCTRINE 8: Human Resources Enhancement Programs Can Be Deeply Effective in the Long Term by Means of "Fireworks Displays" of Extensive Motivational Promotional Displays Seasoned with Regular Doses of Executive Management Speech Making

However, the necessary condition for success of these programs is that there is significant improvement in operating practices by the company so that employees can use what has been talked about and promoted. In other words, employees must actually return to jobs that permit them to *apply* what they have heard. Otherwise, employees will continue to be faced with the same ambiguous management processes that have dominated the working problems they are trying to solve but cannot really influence. And employees will continue to try to thread their way through organizations that are still a group of separate department islands without bridges among them.

WORN-OUT DOCTRINE 9: The Only Truly Primary Areas for Direct Executive Attention Are Likely to Involve Competitive Leadership in Its Highly Visible Form, That Is, between the Company's Products and Services and Those of Its Competitors

It is of course essential that the management team be highly skilled in the company's products and services as well as those of competitors. However, it is also essential that they be familiar with leading an invisible but nonetheless equally potent form of competition—that is, between the company's *working patterns* and the working patterns of its competitors. Otherwise, the consequence is likely to be departmentalized, sometimes tunnel-visioned, and piecemeal activities, which are likely to have limited effectiveness.

The initiatives are likely largely to exist at secondary and tertiary areas of company organization. These programs develop as some grouping of technical projects and of motivational techniques—but without an articulated, integrated, and continuing general management focus that can create fundamental improvement. In weak companies that urgently require major improvement, the most dangerous time for this is when the objective is to try to get only slightly better in company operations.

WORN-OUT DOCTRINE 10: One Can Spend One's Way into Improvement Leadership Results with the Primary Emphasis on Financial Capital Alone

Some of the once-stronger companies recognize that their own decline in market share and profitability began when they substituted large finance-based improvement investment for the approach of also managing smarter by integrating human, physical, and financial factors.

Failed acquisitions, overleveraged mergers, massive reduction of human resources value, and overinvestment in capacity far in excess of market potential are some of the most visible outcomes of this predominating emphasis on financial capital as the center point for growth and profitability. And product technology investment cannot in itself accomplish this growth unless that investment is integrated into a powerful management structure.

CONCLUSION

A continuing and explicit focus on exorcising the outworn management doctrines that can create pockets that work against progress in profitability

CHAPTER 3   EMPHASIZING QUALITY OF MANAGEMENT   55

and growth is one of the key characteristics of the quality of management in today's pacesetter companies. It's an important factor in implementing the experience reported in Chapter 2 of the danger of becoming too fond of—and sticking too long with—business leadership initiatives without confirming their continuing payoff. And it's an important dimension of the character of a company which will be discussed in the next chapter.

CHAPTER 4

THE CHARACTER OF THE COMPANY: "SIGNATURE" CAPABILITIES AND MANAGEMENT INNOVATION

A COMPANY'S CHARACTER IS THE COLLECTIVE RESULT of the business's actions—certainly the actions of the company's management. Sometimes this character includes quality-of-management attributes such as the passion, populism, and disciplined responsibility discussed in Chapter 3. A company's character defines its culture. Employees understand it (even if they cannot always articulate it), astute investors try to employ it as an important factor in their investment decisions, and experienced customers can sense it when they make repeat buying decisions.

Business is about timing. It's affected by the timing of customer expectations, market conditions, financial developments, and management and human resource trends. Because business problems and opportunities, like bananas, generally come in bunches, a company seldom has the luxury to take management action by trying to solve one problem at a time or deal with one opportunity at a time. Instead, what sets the pacesetters apart is their systematic and organized basis for taking management action to deal with the aggregate of their problems and opportunities.

A company's character—and the culture that nourishes it—changes in response to the constantly evolving demands of a churning business world. That character strengthens or weakens as a business's actions lead or instead only react to those demands. A company's speed and effectiveness of action depend on how well the entire company is systematically connected with those demands so that it can execute and implement actions quickly and strongly rather than having to wait for bureaucratic decisions to trickle down.

Experience over the last several years demonstrates that company *size* is not the primary driver of this speed and effectiveness. It does not matter whether a company is large or small. Instead, the driver is the *networking* and *diffusion* of responsibility, understanding, commitment, and execution and implementation throughout the organization to pace and guide its business growth. The attitude is that we will successfully implement and work our way through the business conditions (and of course a good market will help). Together, the networking and diffusion of responsibility and this attitude provide rapid and effective customer and market implementation of the company's hard and soft resources, management doctrines, and management practices and their productive integration in accomplishing superior results.

Again, regardless of whether they are large or small, pacesetter companies depend on their management capital emphasis as the foundation guidelines for accomplishing the integration of networking, diffusion, and an implementation and execution attitude throughout the organization.

Without such a foundation and when under stress from either a growing or a declining market, the character and culture of some companies can evaporate like rain puddles in the hot sun. This was, unfortunately, true of some of the dot-com organizations of the past, and it can happen to companies both large and small. It has been reflected in the tendency to confuse the effects of a good *economy* with the effects of good *management.*

COMPETITIVE LEADERSHIP IN ALL PRINCIPAL MANAGEMENT CAPITAL CHANNELS

The center point of the corporate character of pacesetter companies is sustaining and accelerating profitability and growth, focused on the following key performance results:

- Market leadership—through constantly increasing customer satisfaction, together with the continuing product and service innovation that supports this process
- Operating cost leadership in a company's industries and markets—together with the capital asset effectiveness and productivity that make this possible and the opportunity cost realization and failure cost reduction that help realize this leadership
- Human resource effectiveness
- Organization responsiveness—including time-to-market strength
- Close and constructive relationships with business partners—including suppliers
- Rigorous recognition of public, investor, employee, environmental, and safety responsibility

What in particular sets apart this character of pacesetter companies in accomplishing these key performance results is the emphasis those companies place on the competitive power that results from:

- Making management innovation as systematic and as much a business way of life as product development in the company, while simultaneously also
- Recognizing and preserving the competitive strength of the fundamental and unique competitive advantage "signature" capabilities developed over a long period of time—both of systems and processes and of improvement practices.

The attitude and process create the structure and organization for this—not vice versa—and the management capital approach and content and structure to accomplish this varies among companies driven by their history and their markets and their personalities and their requirements.

THE LONG-TERM COMPETITIVE POWER OF "SIGNATURE" SYSTEMS AND PROCESSES: SIX INSTANCES

These "signature" management systems and processes and attitudes have formed the corporate character and culture of some American (and world) long-term business leaders, and they have been a foundation for the success of their business power. Let us consider the following six instances.

General Electric. One instance is the knowledge base, character, and culture-forming action that derived from the finance, accounting, budgeting management, recruiting, training, and leadership processes that have continued to evolve, adapt, and grow in know-how at the General Electric Company. These factors have been one of the principal character-based reasons why AAA-rated GE is the only remaining organization in the original Dow-Jones Index and are among GE's strengths as it confronts today's fluctuating global demands.

Union Pacific. Another instance is the constantly developing transportation management processes that have contained the key knowledge base for the Union Pacific Railroad in serving and satisfying its customers for well over a century. These management processes have been the foundation for Union Pacific's major character and culture; together with other management capital drivers, they are the reasons Union Pacific remains the largest American railroad. These management processes and the company's character and culture are the constant focus of Dick Davidson, its chief executive officer (CEO), and his associates throughout the railroad's geography and organization.

Cummins Engine. An additional significant instance is the product development process disciplines of Cummins Engine, which have been its knowledge-founded base from the early years of the company. Together with other fundamental management capital processes, they are a key area of the leadership of its CEO, Tim Solso, and are networked throughout the organization.

- **Tenneco.** A further instance is how Mike Walsh and Dana Mead (successive former CEOs for Tenneco) employed the corporate global knowledge base of Tenneco, whose major business holdings were in automotive products, chemicals, energy, packaging, specialty materials, minerals, shipbuilding, and agricultural and construction equipment. The company was systematically structured to diffuse its strength globally, in terms of quality, cost, product, and process leadership. This structure and its strong management leadership made Tenneco one of the very few large conglomerates to successfully build a foundation for significantly increasing the business value of many of these holdings as they went forward in their later separate corporate forms. The leadership of Mike Walsh and Dana Mead was an important factor in the genesis of the structure for the use of total resources discussed in Chapter 9.
- **Southwest Airlines.** An additional instance is how customer satisfaction has been a big factor in Southwest Airlines' business growth in the highly competitive airline market. Southwest recognizes that no guidebook rules can project its customer service philosophy as well as its flight attendants can. After all, it is the flight attendants who are most effective in the personal ways in which they connect with their customers. It has been reported that Southwest has specifically made it clear that no employee will ever be punished for using good judgment and common sense when trying to accommodate a customer, no matter what the rules are.
- **Nestle.** It is sometimes speculated that one-third of the global population subsists on rice, one-third on potatoes, and one-third on bread. Because of its deep and constantly replenished knowledge base, which is strongly supported by its global distribution management processes, Nestle has long succeeded in serving diverse markets.

THE COMPETITIVE POWER OF "SIGNATURE" IMPROVEMENT PRACTICES: *MANUFACTURING AND CUSTOMER SATISFACTION*

Enormous competitive advantage also resides in "signature" improvement practices that have become fundamental ways of life in both small and large companies. The "painting the bridge" approach of an industrial and consumer products manufacturer is an example. People throughout the offices and factory of the company review each and every work operation in the business to find ways to improve value and reduce costs, and they do this every year. This review has been described as "painting the bridge" because it is a constant process that "starts back when you get to the other end." This company's management systems and related processes are supported by a management capital framework that helps identify any backward creep slippage from good established processes and practices that have to get back on track; this framework also helps target major improvement areas in those practices and processes. This is an in-line part of *everyone's* job rather than a series of special "staff" projects. Figure 7(*a*) illustrates the management capital emphasis and attitude the company uses continuously to focus this approach.

A significant part of the time of each manager or supervisor is directed toward helping or teaching employees to make these operations surveys as well as helping to assure the early implementation of the corresponding improvements without delay. A scheduled amount of each employee's time is committed to this work, and employees are empowered to immediately make many improvements by themselves, in cooperation with supervisors, with only later approval from "above." This avoids the bureaucratic waiting for approval before one could do anything that characterized the traditional employee "suggestion system" concept.

Figure 7(*b*) illustrates the effect this has on the changing role of supervisors and managers.

Many work processes and jobs throughout this organization achieved an annual improvement of several percent, which provided an enormous compounding increase in organizationwide performance. That improved performance has been a significant corporate advantage in a highly competitive industry that other large companies—and even small and presumably agile companies—have been unable to emulate.

A further example of "signature" improvement practices is in customer satisfaction and its impact on the marketing and sales of this company. It recognizes that traditional strong marketing and sales development succeeds today *only* when it is coupled with deep respect and action, networked throughout the company, that focuses on delivering complete satisfaction for today's almost universally well-informed customers. This is true for both business and consumer buyers. Customer development and satisfaction cannot be defined or confined to marketing and sales or to rigid administrative procedures. Instead, the emphasis is on the recognition that the men and women in the company must work very hard to understand what their customers' constantly changing wants and needs are *before* they

Figure 7(a) Management Capital–Supported Improvement-Driven Employee Involvement and Empowerment

- Employee involvement and empowerment is both a top-down and a bottom-up process.

- Value-increasing improvement is everybody's job, but it will become nobody's job without management capital support by the establishment of clear customer and supplier-connected management operating systems and work processes that everyone in the organization understands, believes in, is part of, and is helped by.

- This makes value improvement integral to each job, not a separate incident.

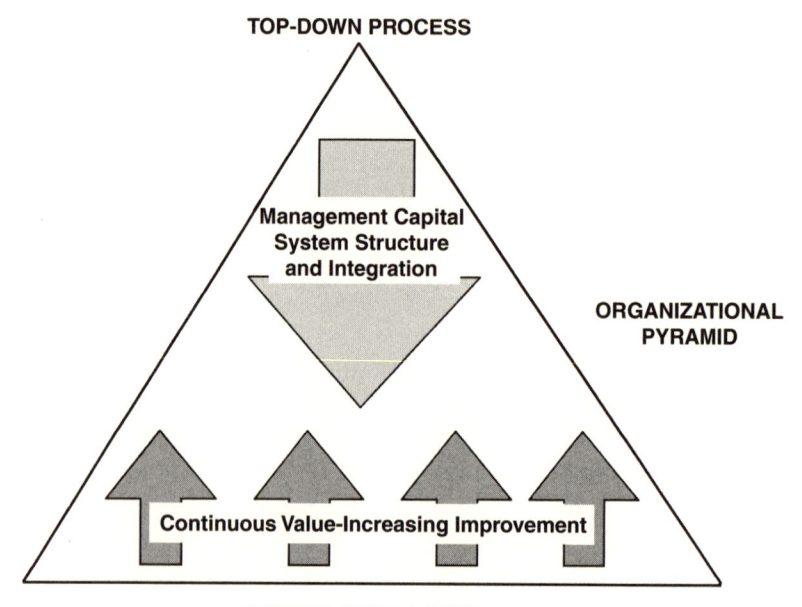

TOP-DOWN PROCESS

Management Capital System Structure and Integration

ORGANIZATIONAL PYRAMID

Continuous Value-Increasing Improvement

BOTTOM-UP PROCESS

THE MANAGEMENT CAPITAL SYSTEMS AND WORK AND TEAM WORK PROCESSES MAKE POSSIBLE

- Working to a common road map
- Communicating
- Understanding what is expected
- Participating in the change process
- Committing to the changes

sell to those customers. Then they must work very hard to respond to those wants and needs as they are diffused through the people who are as close as possible to the buyer. Finally, there is an emphasis on the organizationwide network of genuine support that provides the strength, confidence, and attitude that make customer satisfaction possible.

Figure 7(b)   Management Capital's Changing Role of Supervisors

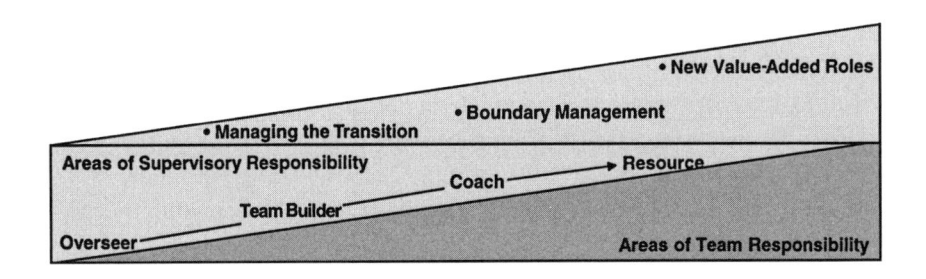

SUPERVISOR-CENTERED   TEAM-CENTERED

- New Value-Added Roles
- Boundary Management
- Managing the Transition

Areas of Supervisory Responsibility

Coach → Resource

Team Builder

Overseer   Areas of Team Responsibility

THE COMPETITIVE POWER OF MANAGEMENT INNOVATION: *MARKETING EFFECTIVENESS*

Our experience shows that continuous systematic management innovation not only is a significant competitive strength for long-term pacesetter companies but also can become one for companies whose business results have been less continuous and are supported much less by signature capabilities.

An example of this is in the marketing effectiveness management channel of a generally very successful major business services corporation with a high degree of cross-selling among its several service segments. After a long period as the industry leader in some of these business segments, the company's results in consumer acquisition and retention had been worsening significantly, market share had been dropping, costs had been increasing, and customer dissatisfaction had been rising.

To help restore its forward momentum and buttress its industry leadership, the company began to emphasize significant management innovation initiatives to provide the competitive power for rebuilding account growth. It began by systematically assessing the needs of the entire corporation for directing those initiatives. For example, one of its key business segments identified the following reasons for the company's downturn:

- It had stayed too long with its existing business tracking processes and its market assumptions in the face of aggressive new competitors.
- It had tried to restore its market position by pushing employees to work harder to succeed, but employee effectiveness was limited by the customer service practices embodied in the existing management

processes and the lack of any innovations that had been initiated in customer service.
- It had been too slow in technology application to its Internet customer access and in its integration of the Web technology and its management processes while at the same time establishing unrealistic expectations for the growth of that business.
- It had allowed its information technology systems pertaining to customer relationships to establish "Rolls Royce" demographics; that is, it had focused much of its service on "big-ticket" customers while taking for granted many other customers who were progressively deserting the company for its competitors. The company failed to recognize that the loyalty factor lasts only as long as customers are being well treated.
- It had largely failed to recognize and identify the fact that the backward business creep in this business segment—whose products had long been a principal factor in the company's cross-selling—had been masked to a great extent by the company's overall strong performance. This was the most significant factor in causing the downturn of this business segment.

These needs became the focus of the company's turnaround plans. The company developed a series of customer and marketing innovation initiatives that were knowledge-based and systematically structured. The goal was to significantly increase

- Customer retention
- Account growth
- Regaining lost customers

These were the three primary factors in accomplishing the following:

1. To better understand and define customer needs by developing highly structured processes for collecting, analyzing, and reporting detailed customer information in order to develop far better real-time knowledge of true customer needs.
2. To connect these customer value needs to the organization's internal capabilities and eliminate customer and company disconnects. This recognized the following four key principles:
    - Regardless of the size of the market, a company acquires customers one at a time.

- It is very hard and costly to acquire customers because of today's constantly changing consumer tastes and because of the fierce competition for satisfying these tastes.
- Therefore, because of the cost of acquiring new customers, it is very important to retain existing customers.
- It is very hard to regain these customers once they have gone to aggressive competitors.

3. To improve customer focus to allow better application of resources and to drive improvements in both product offerings and service processes. Emphasis was placed on a far more nimble organization-wide, customer-focused network. That network had minimal hierarchy, fast decision making, and accelerated action.

Figure 8 reflects one of the continuing process flows for these and other initiatives to systematically emphasize the ongoing competitive power of management innovation.

Taken together, these three objectives provided the foundation for creating the network of processes, tools, resources, and strategies that help, encourage, and connect each person in the organization (both individually and in teams) so that each employee can think, act, and make decisions about how to provide superior performance. Moreover, this network enabled the organization's leadership to provide perceived customer satisfaction throughout the business by delivering consistently improving results.

The effects of these innovations were that caller dissatisfaction decreased significantly throughout all key connections between the organization's employees and their customers; at the same time, total revenue grew substantially over the period.

THE LONG-TERM GLOBAL BUSINESS IMPACT OF MANAGEMENT INNOVATION AND ITS "TEMPORARY MONOPOLY"

When Lawrence Summers was secretary of the treasury, he emphasized the importance of management innovation by pointing out that the American economy is increasingly based on the production of knowledge as well as physical goods. Therefore, the American economy rewards businesses that innovate quickly and grab the largest possible market before being pushed aside by further innovation. Summers said that "the constant pursuit of that temporary monopoly power becomes the central driving thrust." He also quoted Joseph Schumpeter, the great twentieth-century

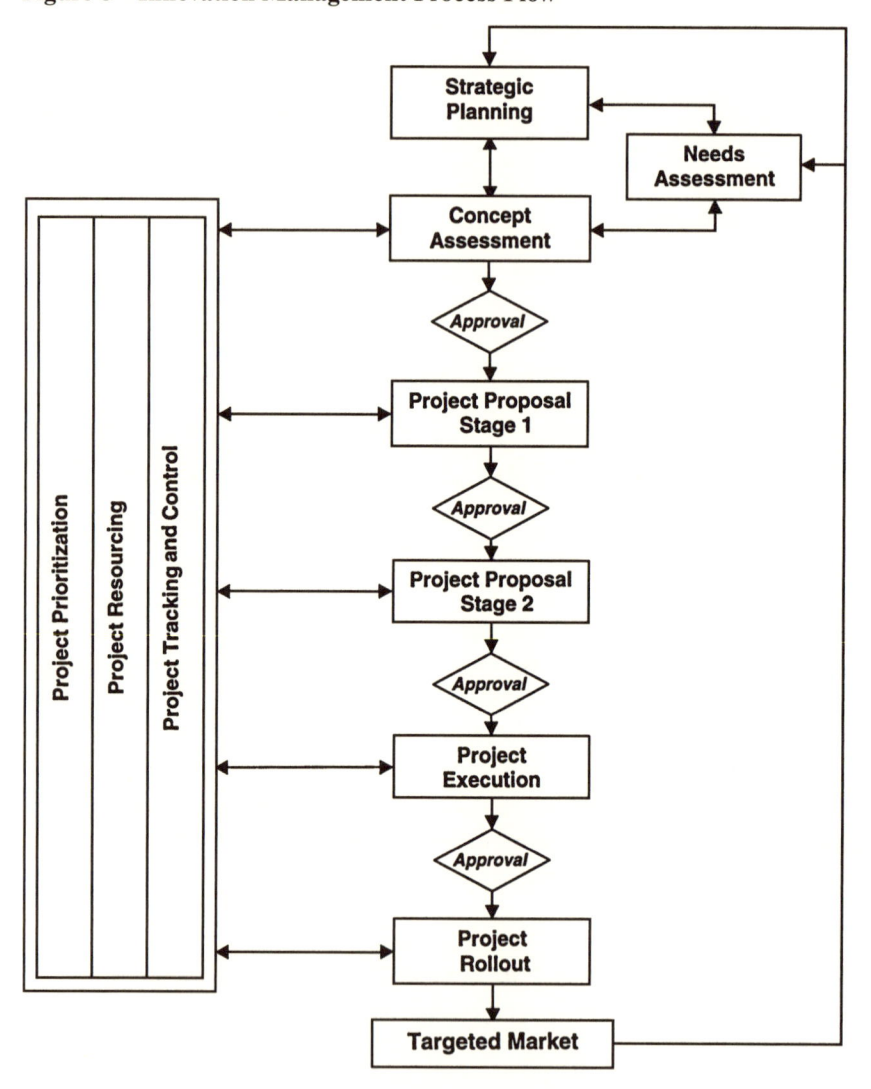

Figure 8 Innovation Management Process Flow

```
                    ┌──────────────────┐
                    │    Strategic     │◄─────────────────┐
                    │    Planning      │                  │
                    └────────┬─────────┘                  │
                             │                            │
                             ▼         ┌──────────────┐   │
                    ┌──────────────────┐│    Needs    │◄──┤
              ┌────►│     Concept      │◄┤ Assessment │   │
              │     │   Assessment     │ └──────────────┘  │
              │     └────────┬─────────┘                   │
              │              ▼                             │
              │          <Approval>                        │
              │              │                             │
┌──────────┐  │              ▼                             │
│ Project  │  │     ┌──────────────────┐                   │
│Prioriti- │  │◄───►│ Project Proposal │                   │
│ zation   │  │     │     Stage 1      │                   │
│          │  │     └────────┬─────────┘                   │
│ Project  │  │              ▼                             │
│Resourcing│  │          <Approval>                        │
│          │  │              │                             │
│ Project  │  │              ▼                             │
│Tracking  │  │     ┌──────────────────┐                   │
│ and      │◄─┤────►│ Project Proposal │                   │
│ Control  │  │     │     Stage 2      │                   │
└──────────┘  │     └────────┬─────────┘                   │
              │              ▼                             │
              │          <Approval>                        │
              │              │                             │
              │              ▼                             │
              │     ┌──────────────────┐                   │
              │◄───►│     Project      │                   │
              │     │    Execution     │                   │
              │     └────────┬─────────┘                   │
              │              ▼                             │
              │          <Approval>                        │
              │              │                             │
              │              ▼                             │
              │     ┌──────────────────┐                   │
              └────►│     Project      │                   │
                    │     Rollout      │                   │
                    └────────┬─────────┘                   │
                             ▼                             │
                    ┌──────────────────┐                   │
                    │ Targeted Market  │───────────────────┘
                    └──────────────────┘
```

economic development thinker: "[T]he creative destruction that results from all that striving becomes the essential spur of economic growth."

Management innovation, together with the much more widely recognized product technology innovation, sums up much of the key force of this business impact for the twenty-first century. This is similar to the way in which the global cycles of management innovation-driven business leadership were galvanized throughout the twentieth century. Consider the following examples:

- The standards approach of Frederick Taylor revolutionized American industrial effectiveness at a time when a combination of production demands driven by World War I and a large and willing but predominantly low-skilled workforce was connected by it.
- Shortly thereafter the charting" and planning approaches of Gantt and others began to establish a systematic foundation to process informal management and helped accelerate output and efficiency.
- The economic boom of the 1920s was measured and clarified by the new emphasis on increasingly structured cost accounting influenced by the early developments of McKinsey and others.
- In the 1930s and 1940s the work measurement principles of Henri Fayol in France came to influence French and European industry and, in their more benign form, some of American industry.
- The principles characterized by National Cash Register's William Patterson and then greatly accelerated and improved by IBM's Thomas Watson changed the meaning of that concept of "sales" supported by an organizational culture and identity and a lifetime human commitment that underpinned it with an emphasis on customer relations that could create a dependable installed customer base.
- The post–World War II business growth, when the United States produced more than two-thirds of the world's output, was strongly influenced by corporate concepts and management principles, guided by the organizational and structural disciplines often associated with Alfred P. Sloan and by the formalized strategic planning activities that were one of their consequences.
- The growth of business leadership in Germany in the 1970s was strongly driven by the revival or development of several management approaches. Those approaches ranged from codetermination by both workers and management to the reemphasis of the "meister" type of front-line management and supervision.
- The return of American business power in the 1980s was assisted and influenced by such management innovations as total quality management and the application of Japanese innovations such as lean manufacturing and just in time and, beginning in the early 1990s, by such guideposts as the Baldrige Award and the progressively more rapid American management innovations discussed in earlier chapters.

- Throughout the 1990s, acceleration in the Internet and information technology reflected a major impact on such areas as enterprise resource planning, the underpinning of supply chain management, customer relationship tracking, and business-to-business partnering.

The character and culture of the companies that were involved in those innovations—and that had the structure and hard- and soft-asset capability for being "early movers" to initiate and implement these innovations—provided a major early competitive and profitability advantage for those companies. Many of those companies continued to maintain that advantage by retaining the relevant "signature" capability that arose from being one of the original early movers while remaining positioned for leadership in the next wave of innovation.

As was discussed in Chapter 2, the key to this leadership is meeting the considerable challenge of systematizing management capital as one of the overarching themes that guide corporate action and as a fundamental way of managing as a corporate way of life and a corporate mindset. This challenge is correspondingly a principal competitive business leadership opportunity and a requirement for success in the twenty-first-century company. The corollary is that systematizing and making technology and the corresponding product development such a way of life and mindset—much more than a "research and development laboratory" and much more than a periodic flash or revelation—was one of the leadership success areas that differentiated twentieth-century corporate leaders from their competitors.

Accomplishing this explicit identification of management capital as the "overarching theme" for management innovation, fully as much as it is for product innovation, requires recognizing the fundamental difference directed toward change. The difference lies in creating a single large improvement and making a career of maintaining it as compared and contrasted with establishing the company's management capital capability for relentlessly continuing competitive leadership growth of management systems and process leadership.

THE CHARACTER OF LEADERSHIP FOR SUSTAINING AND ACCELERATING PROFITABLE BUSINESS GROWTH

In conclusion, several elements of leadership character stand out in pacesetter companies:

1. They lead with a fundamentally new competitive combination of passion, populism, and disciplined responsibility that is reflected in

a bias for action with a hands-on focus because a company's culture for improvement is defined by its actions for improvement and emphasis on widespread communication.

2. They connect the company with the here-and-now business environment: global markets, customer developments, employee attitudes, supplier trends, and investor and public expectations.
3. They establish a clear overview and concept of the company that focuses the organization on its markets and customers.
4. They see their jobs as the acceleration of value for customers, investors, employees, suppliers and other business partners, and the public by relentlessly delivering consistently improving business results.
5. They emphasize that "market-driven" means that their quality is what their *customers*—not what the *company*—says it is and that "affordable quality" means continuously increasing the number of things that have gone *right* for the customer, not just reducing the number of things that have gone *wrong*.
6. They bring back the fizz—i.e., the enthusiasm for working in the organization—through their deep commitment to and belief in the fundamental business improvement by the company employees that comes from their knowledge, skills, and attitudes about solving problems democratically, about the value of teamwork. They understand that *employee* satisfaction correlates directly with *customer* satisfaction.
7. They emphasize the great power of information technology and the Internet both for product and process development and for management itself.
8. They recognize that their sustained growth demands the combination of all the following factors, all the time:
    - Market leadership through constantly increasing customer satisfaction together with continuing product and service innovation
    - Operating cost leadership in their industry and markets, together with the capital assets effectiveness that makes this possible
    - Human resource effectiveness
    - Organization responsiveness, including time-to-market strength

- Close integration with the supplier base
- Rigorous recognition of public, environmental, and safety responsibility

9. They make management innovation as systematic and as much a business "way of life" as product development, while preserving the unique signature capabilities that set the company apart.

They implement these results through effectiveness in developing and deploying management capital's intellectual, technical, human, informational, and other resources in integrating the company's "hard" and "soft" assets. This takes place through the processes, tools, and strategies that help each person in the company think, learn, act, and make decisions about how he or she—both individually and as part of a team—can help provide the superior value to customers and, consequently, to investors that meets today's accelerating business demands.

CHAPTER 5

MANAGING FOR GROWTH IN THE NEW COMPETITIVE LANDSCAPE

CHAPTER 3 EMPHASIZED that the quality of management is the key to sustaining profitable growth and that the twenty-first-century business environment is the incubator of major opportunities for that kind of growth. The power of management capital is that it provides the overarching company theme for empowering this business result amid the brutally competitive demands of the global marketplace, which has transformed some blue-chip companies that were not responsive to these opportunities into "buffalo-chip" companies.

The volatility of this marketplace has created one of the most turbulent economic periods in business history, with enormous change in the economic landscape. The current economy is marked by enormous business change; the speed, aggressiveness, volume, and agility of competition; the almost universal availability of information; and massive mergers, demergers, alliances, and business partnerships of corporate interests.

In the face of these economic cross-currents, management attitude and vision in an increasing number of pacesetting companies have been changing dramatically. Whereas traditionally many managers believed that "it takes a good market for us to grow the business powerfully," they now emphasize that "we'll develop the total opportunity-driven capability for sustaining and accelerating profitable growth for our company by *managing* our way through the conditions we must expect—and good markets will of course help enormously." In other words, fact-based understanding and decision making have become the theme at pacesetter companies.

At the same time, it has become clear that business success in this environment requires a company to develop the winning combination of a clear grasp of the key business factors that are required for strong growth and a relentless capability for recognizing and implementing the new leadership handles that sustain that growth. Understanding and responding to the demands of the globalizing marketplace technology are particularly critical.

HOW THE GLOBALIZING MARKETPLACE IS CHANGING THE WAY BUSINESSES ARE MANAGED

Customer expectations and tastes have been changing quickly because fewer people around the world are willing to accept being second-class or third-class indefinitely—not only in their lives in general but with respect to the products they buy, the services they use, and their working practices. The Internet is rapidly becoming a way of *managing* as well as the consumer's "self-service" *method of choice* for making judgments about products and services, and consumers increasingly bypass many of the information and sales channels on which companies have long based their marketing and customer relations management.

Furthermore, although financial capital markets remain subject to enormous fluctuations, they continue to provide a level of flexibility and availability that has seldom before been available to underwrite growth. And millions of people who only a few years ago lived in directed economies have moved from a cold war atmosphere to a hot business world environment, with the explosive social and economic changes this is bringing about—from the culture of production and sales to the mobility of populations.

For example, quality is becoming an international business language rather than a technical specialty. Investment policy and the expectations of millions of new investors are becoming a combination of mathematical application and a powerful voice in corporate business policy rather than traditional passive acceptors of risk.

Trade barriers are being challenged as more than a billion consumers buy in different forms of common markets and trading zones throughout the world. National and regional economies in various parts of the world—from Asia to Latin America—are increasingly integrated with the United States, Europe, and Japan, and there is an enormous demand for business globalization, although one must recognize the currency and economic fluctuations and other risks that this entails.

The globalization that has been opening new markets ranging from the developing eastern European economies to Asia and particularly China has created an enormous degree of volatility that has driven companies to maintain or lower prices, continue to manage wages carefully, and drive up productivity to grow profitability. In addition, the almost immediate shifting of funds has caused (for example, in the United States) offshore investors to greatly increase or reduce their U.S. Treasury bond holdings, and this has had a major effect on interest rates and the exchange level of the dollar.

Moreover, lending to companies—both established firms and technology start-ups—can greatly accelerate because of the capability of financial markets to offer variable cost alternatives, which provides more possibilities for companies to acquire additional funding, but with far greater risk showing up in equity and bond market fluctuations. Deregulation has injected new issues into the economy, particularly in the telecommunications, utilities, and financial industries which are now re-examining and refocusing upon the sometimes traumatic effect of such deregulation.

HOW STRATEGIC ALLIANCES ARE CHANGING THE COMPETITIVE LANDSCAPE

A further major characteristic of this twenty-first-century business environment is the recognition by many companies of the necessity, in the face of all these cross-currents, to implement their attitude of sustaining growth by creating greater competitive capability through allying with organizations that provide these capabilities despite recognition that a high proportion of such alliances have not worked out.

These are major moves for the consolidation of control and ownership, and they place correspondingly enormous management capital demands on the timely focusing of resources to achieve the merger business objectives. Recognizing the often multinational requirements for merger approval—and accomplishing this in shorter times than was the case formerly—is essential for merger success today because the income needed for this ultimately comes from the customer.

Another and extremely powerful change in this environment is the explosion of forms of business relationships that are very different from the trade merger and acquisition pattern. The corporate objective is to bring about alliances by developing powerful forms of cooperation with organizations that provide competitive capabilities. These require forms of integration for these relationships that are completely different from what is required by management based on ownership and control.

Among the many examples are the objective and the form of General Motor's alliances on its Trade Xchange Web site with what John F. Smith, Jr., GM's chairman, had termed "the GM Group." This group was reported to include Isuzu Motor Co. and Suzuki Motor Co., along with similar alliances with Fuji Heavy Industries and possibly Toyota Motor Co. and Honda Motor Co., with which GM has cooperation deals. Smith explained that GM would focus on this alliance strategy as it attempted to build its business around the world. Of course, these *alliances* are quite different from *acquisitions*, which require fundamental changes in control and ownership. Smith's statement emphasized this distinction: He stated that "each side brings unique advantage to the other, and each side retains its own identity and continues to pursue its own business vision and objectives." Similarly, among others, Ford, Renault, and Daimler-Chrysler individually had also been pursuing such an alliance strategy.

Similar developments have been taking place through many other forms of alliances, for example, when larger companies acquire minority stakes in small companies. This is a growing trend, particularly in big companies that buy significant quantities of equipment (such as software or other components) from smaller companies. Similar trends are occurring in research and marketing agreements that involve *cooperation* but certainly *not control and ownership*, particularly in areas of development where a few years ago a major company would instead have made an acquisition. This is particularly true in the pharmaceuticals and biotech industries.

An equally important trend is the development of relationships for particular purposes between companies that are otherwise strong competitors in their major markets. One of the many examples was the multibillion-dollar arrangement between Acer of Taiwan and IBM for the mutual supply of personal computer (PC) parts while those companies also strongly competed with each other.

What these trends are showing is that in the twenty-first century the old business concept that single, long-term business management models should fit all situations for a company is no longer the pattern (if, in fact, it ever really was). Not only are management innovations for the business models becoming a major competitive focus and company asset, the leadership and management demands for these alliance models are far different from those for the twentieth-century model, which was based on the *hierarchy* of ownership and control rather than on *networking* it. The effectiveness of a company's management-capital theme and attitude becomes even more important for achieving the intended integration and confluence of the allying companies' capabilities—even more important than integrating companies' capabilities when a company executes a traditional ownership consolidation or merger.

The character of the challenge is demonstrated by such statistics as those which have demonstrated that 70 percent of mergers have *not* produced effective results.

HOW THE USE *AND* MANAGEMENT OF TECHNOLOGY PROVIDE COMPETITIVE ADVANTAGE

As was discussed earlier in this book, today's information, software, communications, and Internet technologies are comparable in their power for creating major new business opportunities to the general-purpose technologies (such as electricity, automobiles, telephones, radio, and aircraft, among others) that characterized other major growth periods in business history. Such technology is the foundation not only for creating major *new* products but also for providing much greater effectiveness in the development and productivity of *existing* products. For example, although the Internet is primarily a business *product* center point for Cisco, it is also a business *effectiveness capability* for that company. For General Electric, it is primarily a business effectiveness capability, but it also has growing potential as an important component of such offerings as GE's medical products.

Not too long ago technology was a primary business differentiator that was literally "owned" by some companies (such as Xerox in reproduction and DuPont and Bayer in chemicals and pharmaceuticals) and by some geographic regions (such as Japan in consumer electronics). In contrast to those earlier business periods, however, in the twenty-first century technology no longer travels under any single (or even two or three) corporate or national passports and does not have any particular cultural or social identity. Instead, innovative technology-based products and services that once would have provided a long exclusive life to the producing company are now commoditized by competitors with frightening speed. Today the corporate differentiator lies in *what the company can do* with technology, that is, how the company is clearly and inspirationally directed by its customers and markets, as well as how quickly it integrates its technology innovations throughout its total business structure instead of merely developing new technologies in a traditional "research laboratory" or development functional silo.

In other words, in this era of technology and product proliferation, technology generates its full power *only* when the effectiveness of a company's *product technology capability* is matched by the effectiveness of its *business leadership capability:* its management innovations and its constancy of management capital.

THE DEMAND TO BE A MARKET LEADER

The first part of this chapter described this competitive landscape marked by such forces as global markets, alliances, and technology. The purpose of that discussion was to set the stage for a description of how companies around the world have been trying to continue to transform themselves dramatically in ways that can meet these demands for rapid change and significant improvement.

This is an environment in which being a leader is the key to achieving the important business rewards in market share and profitability. It has been described as a "winner-takes-all" business environment—certainly with the objective of being number one or number two—because success begets success. This objective demands rigorous maintenance, in accordance with the attitude and vision of today's pacesetters that "we'll effectively lead and manage the total company resources to realize our opportunities."

This attitude and vision is particularly evident in the e-business and e-commerce arena and in the bloodbath results of the many dot-coms that unfortunately were unable to make the cut. The strong first-mover companies (such as auctioneer E-Bay's potential strength in fighting against the incursion of larger rivals) focus on rigorous maintenance of their processes for availability of both the best selection of products and the best customer traffic. Similarly, because most markets can support only two or three leaders and brands, Amazon.com's relentless drive into profitability depended on building both brand and market share.

THE IMPROVEMENT IMPERATIVE IN THE NEW COMPETITIVE LANDSCAPE

These pressures in this new competitive landscape and the need to respond to them to sustain and accelerate profitability and growth have created new demands throughout the business value chain of companies both large and small. The reason is clear: All of these changes, taken together, gradually create enormous change in customer expectations, employee attitudes, international growth, and cost trends. Some companies that *seem* to be doing well can nonetheless become progressively (although almost imperceptibly) more and more *disconnected* from these fundamental drivers of their business strength. This disconnect becomes quickly apparent when the economic demand changes rapidly.

These companies may be continuously successful for some period of time, but they nonetheless can be progressively growing out of touch with these rapid changes in business globalization, new markets, new employee attitudes, and new management approaches. They may not have fully recognized early on, as pacesetter companies had done, how big these changes have been and how fundamental their own management changes need to be. Our data show that this is reflected in the creation of major competitive opportunities for continuing management innovation in many areas throughout the business value chain.

The following sections describe nine areas of such opportunities to improve competitive position.

GLOBAL EXPANSION

While many companies have been strongly penetrating world markets, some companies have evolved their international businesses as a group of separate, largely unconnected silos. They have not fully used their growing international size as a strength. This makes them unnecessarily vulnerable to the volatility of today's global markets compared with competitors that have sharply increased their international earnings by systematically making their best operative practice *anywhere* quickly available *everywhere* throughout their global businesses, and have correspondingly also established strong local national relationships and strengths.

TIME CYCLE COMPRESSION

The time needed to deliver a product or service to customers from the moment an order is received is still too long in many companies because of the circuitous order fulfillment route even when that route is dramatically improved by information technology. Leading companies make a central strategic initiative of aggressively moving toward consistent, period-by-period reduction by relentlessly eliminating the disconnects in this cycle time. This timesaving initiative also results in substantial cost savings as well as greatly improved customer satisfaction.

CUSTOMER SATISFACTION

The gap between company and buyer perceptions of customer satisfaction continues to grow in many markets. This is reflected in the divergence between company *data* on customer satisfaction and *actual* customer reactions. Company data on customer satisfaction often show that defects have been reduced and features have been increased, for example, in the technology used in financial services. However, customer *reaction* itself may indicate that satisfaction is in fact lower because of perceived lower product (or service) value and affordability.

MANAGING INFORMATION TECHNOLOGY

In spite of the great business value of information systems, their installation and management often have been characterized by large-scale cost and time loss consequences. Some studies have shown that up to 70 percent of installations have been affected in this way. The more systems have been added, the more dedicated resources have often been needed. Managing the continuing *process* changes to facilitate successful *system* installation is a major issue in ensuring a favorable impact on business results.

PRODUCT AND SERVICE INNOVATION
To combat rapid product commoditization by competitors, leadership companies are developing and distributing new products or services through a sequence of major improvement initiatives to reduce huge costs and new product vulnerability to nimble competitors.

SUPPLY MANAGEMENT
Although there has been significant improvement in supply integration compared with the take-the-baseball-bat-to-suppliers approach of some companies in the past, there remain enormous new partnering opportunity for time, cost, and delivery cycle reduction improvement in many businesses.

QUALITY
Despite widespread efforts to improve quality, quality failure costs are still very high at many companies even after substantial improvements. The quality "distance" (i.e., the difference in the level of quality that consumers now expect and the quality level that companies are actually delivering) between some companies and their customers has in fact increased in some areas—creating great opportunity and demand for improvement.

ASSET MONETIZATION
Companies of course acquire facilities—i.e., land, buildings, and equipment—originally intended for specific business purposes. Unfortunately, during the changing demands of the last decade some facilities progressively came to be used unproductively. However, they remain on the books of some companies because of a lack of focused and coordinated processes for making meaningful divestiture decisions.

ENVIRONMENTAL DEMANDS AND RISK MANAGEMENT
To meet stringent environmental regulations, some companies have adopted technologies that are slap-on systems, for example, to treat pollution at the emission point. A more efficient long-term approach *changes the manufacturing process* to eliminate the use of harmful chemicals or to install front-end technologies that treat pollution at the source. Only some companies have moved in this direction even though failure to do so can represent a long-term financial risk for them.

THE INTERNET IS A DIGITIZED OPPORTUNITY FOR MANAGEMENT INNOVATION: FIVE KEY E-TECHNOLOGY APPLICATION AREAS

In addition to the nine management challenges just described, a tenth major opportunity is increasingly serving these challenges (and many others): The Internet is a key enabler for companies that are developing their management capital and implementing systematic and continuing management innovation. At the same time, the Internet is a major, growing force for companies that are trying to improve the use of their total resources and connect their hard and soft assets in order to accelerate business results.

In accomplishing this result, pacesetter companies recognize that although the Internet is the enabler, it is also a technology that is equally available to their competitors with the needed investment capacity. Therefore, when developing their Internet-related management innovation initiatives, pacesetter companies emphasize that their unique competitive strength lies is in how they *manage, lead, and implement* the initiative and its next steps. Furthermore, of particular importance is how effectively these companies develop and install the *processes* that are the foundation for performance improvement.

Five broad areas have proved to be particularly important for successful and continuing digitized management innovation:

1. Manufacturing and production
2. Marketing and sales
3. Supply
4. Malls and exchanges
5. Product development networks for customers, dealers, and user-participants

The rest of this chapter generally discusses the improvement point-of-view for each of these areas.

1. USING E-TECHNOLOGY FOR MANAGEMENT INNOVATION IN MANUFACTURING AND PRODUCTION

One of the most fundamental areas of management innovation in the twenty-first-century company is the use of the Internet as a key to rethinking and reinventing the management of manufacturing throughout the company. The objective is to position the company's movement toward the manufacturing "pull" pattern and away from manufacturing "push." Manufacturing pull connects production directly with the customer, whereas the traditional push method bases production on factory schedules that were established by the company's *estimates* of customer demand in terms of volume, product mix, and other requirements. More important, companies that managed in terms of push manufacturing experienced the following business problems: big inventories; long cycle times; and relationships with parties ranging from suppliers to dealers and distributors that were almost constantly in flux—all of which caused problems in sales volume and cost increases.

For example, in the automotive industry studies have shown that as many as half the prospective customers in car dealer showrooms do not find the car configuration that they want. One result of push production management is that a predetermined mix of cars is built and shipped to dealers who sell them or have to be part of rebate schemes to move the product. This has created what at one time was an estimated $60 billion of completed vehicle inventory in the U.S. market and an approximate 60-day (or more) average time from customer order to delivery. High inventories are one of the principal reasons why major automotive companies have made it clear that moves to pull manufacturing should lead to substantial reductions in average order-to-delivery time and completed vehicle inventory.

2. USING E-TECHNOLOGY FOR MANAGEMENT INNOVATION IN MARKETING AND SALES

A second fundamental area of management innovation is a focus on integrating e-technology with marketing and sales to create new management capabilities for profitable growth in business volume. One key objective is effectively structuring the customer self-service purchasing capability for a company's product and service buyer.

Marketing experience is demonstrating that this is a way in which many twenty-first-century customers like to buy and that this buying method actually contributes to greater customer satisfaction. This is the case because customers can enter their own orders, browse through catalogs, compare competitive price and value information, and find solutions to their problems. Internet buying has been reinventing the customer-oriented marketing and sales management process for some companies and has put great emphasis on better sales and marketing discipline for many businesses.

The reason for this is that the initial impact of sales management of Internet-driven e-business and e-commerce is that it makes a company's quality value quickly transparent to the company's customers and to everybody else. Because it is the buyers' self-service method of choice for making judgments about products and services, Internet shopping increasingly bypasses the information, quality, and marketing channels through which companies have judged and packaged marketing intelligence about how customers react to a company's products.

Experience is showing that in some markets, when companies structure *how they manage* the Internet with the *processes* to provide immediately high quality and customer satisfaction (so that customers are happy), customers are likely to buy more at a time in online transactions than they did before and are more likely to come back regularly to that site. This provides the possibility of providing the company with very lucrative, high-purchase-size sales. It also shows that these are the tough customers who set a high bar that a company has to recognize and cross to get profitably into the big market volume of the future.

Internet marketing and sales can build brand identity powerfully. It can also lower marketing and sales expenses so that only two or three companies (at most) are likely to make it big in any online market. Therefore, moving fast is essential. Moreover, Internet marketing and sales can cut production costs, cycle time, and inventories. Correspondingly, if companies do not manage online marketing and sales properly—i.e., if they generate customer *dissatisfaction* and *errors*—the word gets around so fast that buyers can tank a company's click operations far more quickly than they ever could destroy an Old Economy company's brick operations.

These customers also provide companies with a very important database for determining how Internet markets are likely to develop in the next two or three years. When a company can get a fix on its Internet customers' demographics, it can start to build a good foundation for understanding the basic factors of the momentum that is likely to drive its Internet markets and the sales that move in them.

All this is enormously important to making a success of the management innovation with this e-technology emphasis, because the first-mover company is likely to remain the long-term winner in online marketing. For instance, E-Bay's one-year head start in auctions over Yahoo continued to provide it with market share leadership because buyers are likely to want to stay where other buyers are in these markets and vice versa.

3. USING E-TECHNOLOGY FOR MANAGEMENT INNOVATION IN SUPPLY

A third fundamental area of management innovation is supply. This area has an enormously important impact on business results in terms of product volume, cycle time, mix, and quality. Using the Internet for supply also places new demands on communications and process development, fully as much as it does on the parts and materials themselves. Consumer merchandising is one of the key example areas.

One important pacesetter is Wal-Mart, whose profitability and growth reportedly are being driven strongly by its management of supply through an Internet-integrated, customer service–based, supplier partnering network. This network gives suppliers a direct connection with Wal-Mart customer sales systems. Essentially, the system enables major suppliers to immediately and directly maintain the supply of the right types and quantity of products and services to Wal-Mart stores.

Because Wal-Mart's Internet network can include links to banks, suppliers now, in principle, can be paid virtually as soon as a customer purchase crosses the checkout bar-code reader. When properly negotiated and partnered, this payment system can be a win-win situation for both Wal-Mart and its suppliers. The system greatly accelerates the immediacy of the suppliers' cash flow; at the same time, volume and prompt payment allow Wal-Mart to demand bigger discounts and reduced retail prices to support its competitive emphasis on what it calls "everyday low prices."

This platform reportedly leverages Wal-Mart into establishing mall sales with the intention of launching new E-Superstore as the company increasingly goes global. This mall exchange has been reported to feature a large number of products and new personalized services and can support many concurrent online buyers with pacesetting new technology. Its design objective is to further grow Wal-Mart's sales by combining its strength of many brick-and-mortar stores with the convenience of this online shopping mall by providing the buyer with the option of picking up or returning merchandise either online or at a local store. It also provides an Internet product add-on to Wal-Mart's already well-established capability in photofinishing. Using the E-Superstore's new photo center, customers can view their photos online, print photos to any store around the world, and e-mail photos to family and friends.

Finally, the Internet supply system is intended to provide a great service to Wal-Mart customers by providing availability of banking and travel centers, with great value also to Wal-Mart's supplier partners in these areas.

4. USING E-TECHNOLOGY FOR MANAGEMENT INNOVATION IN MALLS AND EXCHANGES

A fourth e-technology management innovation opportunity area is developing malls and exchanges. This innovation can cause two major business results. First, malls and exchanges leverage a company's *brand name* (which generates additional sales); second, they can leverage the company's *buying volume* (which generates more favorable purchase performance). Each of these applications, however, places additional operating requirements on the company's processes. For example, the company must assure the pinpoint accuracy of deliveries demanded by online customers, and it must provide major suppliers with "firewall" protection of their proprietary and pricing information.

5. USING E-TECHNOLOGY FOR MANAGEMENT INNOVATION IN CUSTOMER, DEALER, AND USER-PARTICIPANT PRODUCT DEVELOPMENT NETWORKS

The fifth management innovation area is using the Internet to provide continuing market leadership through strong product development networks with continuing customers, dealers, and user-participants. These networks are connected with company design and manufacturing engineers, dispersed among multiple sites globally. They generate new, already-customer-tested products with much shorter development cycle times and lower production costs to fit today's fast cycle customer self-service market, where new products are being commoditized frighteningly quickly. Another channel of this network provides for almost instantaneous customer and dealer feedback on newly launched products so that immediate adjustments can be made.

CHAPTER 6

SUSTAINING BUSINESS GROWTH BY RECOGNIZING AND RECONNECTING MANAGEMENT "DISCONNECTS"

CHAPTER 5 DESCRIBED HOW THE GLOBALIZING MARKETPLACE and technology—together with alliances, acquisitions, and mergers—have created major competitive leadership opportunities and the management imperative to seize them. It emphasized the importance of why and how pacesetting companies are focusing seminal new strengths of leadership and quality of management to sustain and accelerate profitable growth.

The basic business premise of these leaders is that the competitive forces that have been let loose throughout the world will make the economic demands of the recent past look like merely a warmup practice for the brutal business requirements that will dominate the next three to five years. The management attitude in these companies is emphasizing a complete transformation of the organization from any vestiges of the mentality that "it takes a good market for us to continue to grow the business powerfully." Instead, the mentality that is emphasized is that "we'll successfully *manage* our way to sustain profitable growth for our company throughout whatever set of business conditions there are....and, of course, a good market will help."

RECOGNIZING THE OPPORTUNITIES AND THE DISCONNECTS THAT FACE COMPANIES

This attitude is particularly critical in times like these, which combine unusual economic opportunities with significant business disconnects created by these changing marketplace and technology and acquisition forces.

As was discussed in earlier chapters, pacesetting companies are strongly focusing on *capitalizing their management power* to deal with these challenges. Pacesetter companies develop their market and leadership capabilities and then use those capabilities to systematically develop, operate, measure, and integrate their technology capacities, brand names, customer relationships, human resources, international connections, business processes, supply networks, and quality and service capability. Pacesetters consider all these factors to be as critical as their all-important physical assets and financial capital.

Pacesetting companies are integrating and focusing their full resources (soft as well as hard) in the new management and leadership models with competitively strong infrastructure and with the e-frastructure of the Internet for productivity and growth. Their objective is to ensure the convergence of what has been shown to work best throughout today's marketplace. This is crucial because today's marketplace is one in which networks and diffusion of responsibility work better than bureaucracy, an emphasis on creativity is essential, and the employees who are closest to what is happening are those who can lead and improve it most effectively in a sustained economy.

PREMISES FOR ACTION

Business leaders are grappling with the strategic and operational factors that will transform their companies' effectiveness into this new leadership and management model for seizing these business opportunities. At the same time, these leaders recognize their companies' strengths and vulnerabilities that will either help or hinder their ability to take advantage of those opportunities. To achieve full resource-based results, business leaders have come to recognize five premises underlying the actions they must take:

1. That it is hazardous to assume that leadership and management practices that were highly productive for their companies during the long-running strong economy of the past will be similarly effective in the very different economy of the next several years, especially considering the enormous technological developments that have accompanied this change. This assumption is especially problematic because some of these carryover leadership and management practices are still firmly embedded in the way some companies work.

2. That a fundamental business risk is that these pressures can cause several of a company's management channels to grow out of touch with these changing business requirements (unless there is strong leadership to prevent this).

3. That in today's intensely competitive world the only way you can maintain the momentum and visibility of your business' growth is to extend it relentlessly. Otherwise, it is like the ice on a lake in early spring: It is there in the morning, but by the afternoon it can be gone.

4. That this emphasizes the need to give key areas of the company "a business physical"—a regular review or audit of how these key areas are functioning (which is discussed in detail later in this chapter). The physical is important because the company's leaders have to understand how extensive and fundamental their management innovation needs to be to help employees throughout the company achieve the necessary improvement results.

5. That this is very hard work; indeed, it is one of the fundamental leadership and management jobs in the twenty-first-century company.

BEWARE OF "BACKWARD CREEP" IN CORPORATE PERFORMANCE FROM CARRYOVER BUSINESS ISSUES

All this is amplified by the carryover business issues created by periods of long economic expansion followed by major economic change, such as today's situation. This creates enormous business challenges for companies positioning themselves to make these new opportunities their own. Good business leaders understand that it is when their companies were experiencing major continuing growth and posting increasing earnings (with the corresponding cash flow to fund major improvement), that had been precisely the time to focus on constant, improvement-driven management innovation. Good business leaders understand the economic history that makes it abundantly clear that organizations that relentlessly achieve fundamental business improvement when business is *good* are far better prepared to continue the trend of improvement when business conditions become *difficult*.

However, in those periods when strong markets can reward past performance for a while, there can be great pressure not to "mess with success" and run the risk of interfering with what has been strong performance. When an organization is a continuously very profitable performer and already has a full plate, it can be a lot tougher to build incentive for rigorous improvement—which requires change—than it is in periods when every person working in the organization comes face to face with tough times. The management skills (and even the stomach) to lead such fundamental improvement can sometimes atrophy during a strong up-economy period no matter how many motivational initiatives and widely promoted patterns of executive speech making may be taking place.

This history, combined with large-scale economic change, can create huge new economic pressure on companies that result from today's powerful new business forces. It can be visualized as a competitive scissors whose sharp jaws squeeze down on many companies. One jaw is the strong *upward* pressure on company cost created by the increases companies continue to face in spite of their best cost-containment efforts. The other jaw is the severe *downward* pressure on price created by today's market changes. In some companies this can progressively create what we call "backward creep" in performance. This backward creep is gradually reflected in technology, customer satisfaction performance, employee attitudes, and cost trends. It can take place even if it seems that a company's conformance to existing business practices may be having good results.

For example, backward creep in the *quality* of products and services takes place when companies maintain standards but customer expectations change and technology shifts occur. Companies *adhere* to those internal standards and practices, but they do not systematically and constantly *align* them with these changing customer expectations and technology changes. Therefore, these companies can become increasingly disconnected from customers, with consequent *management* disconnects among the company components that serve and respond to customers.

Although quality control structures and standards are important and necessary, companies may fail to recognize and deal with the problems early enough that arise in a marketplace in which customer expectations are constantly changing and technology is constantly shifting—that holding regular compliance audits with these standards may not guarantee customer satisfaction or loyalty.

Furthermore, backward creep in *effectiveness* is often unmeasured in some companies in critically important management capital channels, including marketing effectiveness, product development, human resources, and technology development. Without analysis, the developing issues may not be recognized as subjects for serious management emphasis until they become serious problems, both large and small.

Without fundamental change toward effectively capitalizing their management power, of course, this is an open invitation to being blindsided by global competitors whose vision had not been similarly clouded by the success dust of an earlier strong growth economy. These competitors have therefore been able to understand and respond to the forces that are defining the genuine opportunities facing their companies.

PRODUCTIVE COST REDUCTION: CONSTANT MANAGEMENT INNOVATION IN ACTION

Cost reduction is one of the most transparent and fundamental examples of quality-of-management leadership in facing and dealing with these issues. Leaders in pacesetter companies should tackle cost reduction by emphasizing a complete business organization network.

In today's economy cost reduction should always be an ongoing discipline. However, when the economy is strong, it is not always easy to maintain the necessary emphasis on keeping costs down. Also, there can be less of an incentive to push hard to change what seems to be a successful business formula of unfocused and intermittent cost reduction.

One of the defining characteristics of today's pacesetter companies is that they emphasize the power of their management capital for strong ongoing business leadership of cost management in good times fully as much as they do in bad times. They systematize cost reduction as a fundamental businesswide way of life. They emphasize consistent attention that concentrates on fundamental improvements in customer, employee, and supplier relationships and on companywide cost planning. These companies succeed because they rigorously plan for and meet the fluctuating demands of business through management innovations that are driven by a cost-reduction program over the complete business cycle.

This approach recognizes the importance of and emphasizes cost reduction day by day, incrementally, and for every technical project undertaken by a company. In other words, this is "continuous improvement" in the traditional specialist staff-led approach of some companies, which is characteristic of the emphasis on cost reduction in those companies during good times. However, without the foundation of basic ongoing management innovation-driven improvement in times of economic stress, business conditions may force these companies to turn to an emphasis on slash-and-burn cost reduction. This can result in discontinuing good product and equipment initiatives or even terminating strong employee relationships. Our experience in accomplishing consistently effective cost reduction productively and systematically in many pacesetting companies makes it clear that significant, ongoing, bottom-line-driven results require cost reduction that is carefully focused. The focus at these companies is on passing four tests to ensure that the company's full resources are used to develop competitively strong, cost-driven management innovation. These four tests are as follows:

1. Is it based on business facts and the use of soft assets as well as being cost-accounting-based? If it is not, companies may miss the big cost-reduction opportunities of today's marketplace. In spite of all these years of accounting practice and of outstanding and continuing efforts to quantify soft and other earnings assets (discussed in earlier chapters), many organizations still do not always know what their true costs are.

2. Is it directed toward improving and using customer, supplier, and other alliance relationships? Is it also improving technology development?

Is it improving the human resources skills that also contribute significant strength to cost-reduction opportunities?
3. Are its results as transparent and motivational as possible in terms of potential benefits for the employees who have to make them happen throughout the business's value chain?
4. Are these cost-reduction results clearly defined in terms of new bottom-line growth opportunities for enhanced service and corporation profitability?

This makes cost reduction an integral part of the business's emphasis on its *management capital attitude* and its *total resource orientation*. It makes cost reduction genuinely productive in all areas, including strong growth in annual sales per employee, reduced costs of delivering complete customer satisfaction, and competitive leadership in the effectiveness of the company's supply chain (which is discussed in more detail later in this chapter). For example, studies indicate that some global business pacesetters that have managed cost reduction this way have seen their annual sales per employee rise by an average of *more than 60 percent* over a period of years.

WHY "SLASH-AND-BURN" IMPROVEMENTS ARE ULTIMATELY INEFFECTIVE

Pacesetter companies recognize an enormous difference between this kind of competitive leadership and that of companies whose approach to cost management, change, and restructuring is based on slash-and-burn improvement. In those companies cost reduction is often "managed" simply by moving business problems from one department to another instead of solving those problems and by emphasizing brain drizzles instead of brainstorms. This approach has not worked because it increases the distance between a company's employees and its customers.

Experience makes it clear that cost reduction should be synchronized with specific improvements in a company's way of working, the way it serves its customers, and the way it integrates its hard and soft assets. If these factors are *not* synchronized, it is like weight reduction without a change in lifestyle—in other words, the good results will not last. Ultimately the company will need to do even more cost reduction; it will have more difficulty dealing with customer market leadership and will be caught in a vicious cycle of having to make the same moves over and over.

Companies operating this way try to achieve *consistent* business improvement with a loose collection of functional silos and management technique projects supported by motivational meetings which have to be repeated under different labels and often with different packaging. The business effectiveness approach of these organizations has sometimes seemed to act like logs floating down a fast-moving river with many hands holding on, each of which thinks it is steering. This approach to business was summed up in a recent two-panel cartoon. The left panel showed a management group sitting around a business table, with the caption reading: "We've just got to restructure and downsize around here." In the right panel, labeled "one year later," the same group is shown around the same table, with the caption reading: "Now that we're restructured, what do we really do differently?"

MANAGEMENT PROBLEMS AT "DISCONNECTED" COMPANIES

These issues have been occurring most heavily in organizations that have been developing broad strategies but whose alignment, integration, and identification of clear business opportunities with this strategy are in fact far too isolated from the rapid changes in the way their customers now actually buy. Moreover, these organizations are not able to use input from employees who directly understand these customers and their demands, therefore limiting the effectiveness of their use of digitized customer data.

In addition, these organizations continue to deal with their suppliers by intimidating them, which obviously is not the *partnering* approach required today. Today's economy demands speed and knowledge integration between companies and their suppliers, with a foundation of good information management process-driven data.

These organizations have intermittent and uncoordinated integration of new technology with product and service performance and operations improvement.

Companies that are disconnected have many problems in the way they manage human resources. Their human resources programs remain keyed to "fireworks displays"—extensive motivational seminars seasoned by regular doses of management speech making and extensive training in improvement techniques—but without an effective *management foundation* to facilitate change. When employees return to their jobs to use what they have heard at seminars, in speeches, or in training sessions, they are still faced with the same unclear management processes that they cannot influence. They still have to try to thread their way through an organization that is a group of separate departmental islands without any bridges. In other words, they still have to deal with the organization's *ambiguity*, which convinces veteran employees that this is just the most recent of the improvement crusades they have seen in their careers, all of which have died and been buried without an autopsy.

These disconnected companies continue to approach employee development with the idea that good human resources management and successful improvement mean effectiveness initiatives that basically get down to "getting the ideas out of the boss's head and into the hands of the workers." This is the kind of worn-out management doctrine discussed in Chapter 3. This fallacy is characterized by an *inward*-looking restructuring that looks at internal corporate initiatives while too often growing out of touch with rapid changes in new markets, new employee attitudes, and new management approaches.

This disconnectedness shows up in companies that experience any or all of the following problems:

- Improvement plans have not been "real."
- Strategy, business plans, and measurements have not been aligned.
- Planning has been primarily financial instead of involving the full hard and soft assets of the business.
- Financial capital allocation has not been systematically related to improvement requirements.
- Improvement plans are isolated and have not incorporated or integrated the full range of modern improvement opportunities from supply to information technology.
- Surprises and counterpunching have kept improvement initiatives unstable.
- Improvement has been organizational but has not necessarily been based on each line of business.
- Technology has not been recognized for its future potential.
- Improvement plans have been one-time activities without continuity.
- Improvement has not had companywide integration in full business terms.
- Resource planning, including human and technology resources, has not been clearly structured.
- Improvement plans have not fully included alternatives to respond to and restore unexpected financial shortfalls.

- Plans have not been developed on a true organizationwide integrated basis so that what works well *anywhere* in the organization has not been made quickly available on a "best practices" basis *everywhere* in the organization.
- Implementation of initiatives has been limited in focus and execution.

These are scenarios a company should try to avoid if it wants its business to stay connected.

HOW DISCONNECTED MANAGEMENT CREATES A "HIDDEN ORGANIZATION"

The impact of these disconnects is especially strong on management itself. For example, Figure 9 shows our data from a cross-section of organizations with these characteristics, specifically, that an enormous amount of their management resource effectiveness is drained from the intended business leadership work because of this "disconnect effect." It creates an unproductive "hidden organization," which is discussed more fully in Chapter 7.

Employees at these organizations are very busy, but they are being "nickel-and-dimed"—i.e., diverted from their goals—by continually trying to patch together and work their way through these disconnects. This situation creates a huge competitive disadvantage that is sensed in these companies but usually is not measured and is dealt with only incrementally.

BUSINESS PROBLEMS CAUSED BY DISCONNECTED MANAGEMENT

In companies that have organization silos the truly primary time-demanding area for direct executive attention is likely to be competitive leadership with respect to a company's products and services. This area usually gets the most attention because the product and service marketplace is so visible. Many managers are increasingly skilled in this highly visible product and service marketplace but have become less familiar with leading the invisible (but nonetheless equally potent) form of competitive strength that concerns leadership in *how the company works*. (This aspect of leadership has been touched on in earlier chapters and will be more fully reviewed in Chapter 8.)

The consequence is likely to be management initiatives that are departmentalized, sometimes tunnel-visioned, and piecemeal. Experience has shown that such initiatives are likely to have only a limited effect on

Figure 9 Disconnect Effect

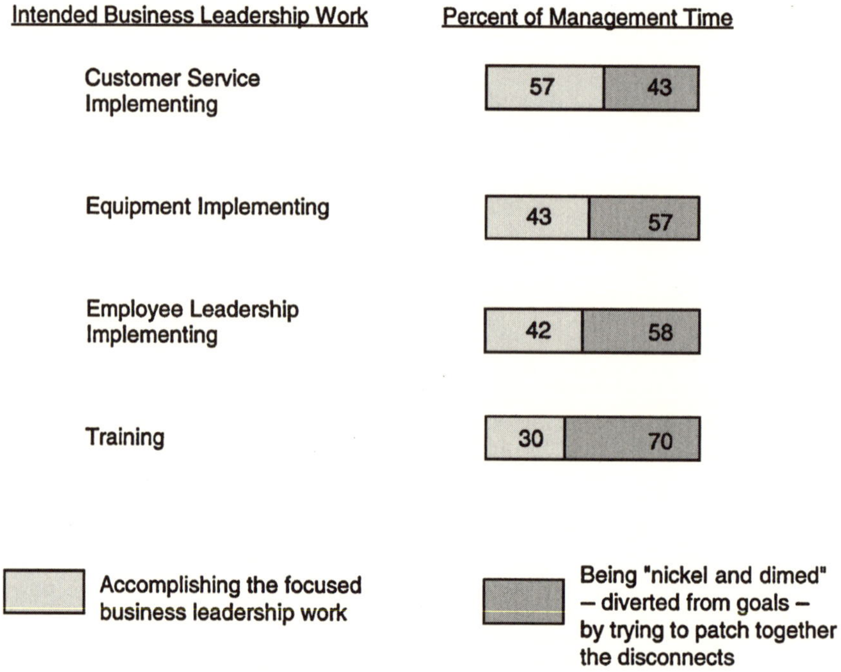

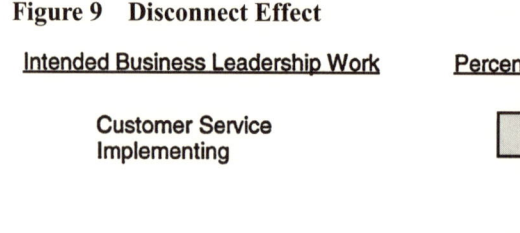

Intended Business Leadership Work	Percent of Management Time
Customer Service Implementing	57 / 43
Equipment Implementing	43 / 57
Employee Leadership Implementing	42 / 58
Training	30 / 70

☐ Accomplishing the focused business leadership work

▓ Being "nickel and dimed" – diverted from goals – by trying to patch together the disconnects

resolving the disconnects. This situation is exacerbated by the unfocused use of key company resources, including the most important resource of any company: the knowledge, skills, learning capacity, and attitude of people throughout the organization.

Although major business effectiveness initiatives are strongly emphasized in these companies, it seems easier to begin them without directly confronting the "culture" of the company's silo-based orientation and to hope for the best in top-to-bottom company impact in the evolution of the major business effectiveness initiatives. However, experience shows that the effectiveness initiatives are likely to continue to develop with an emphasis on essentially functional and technical areas, and the improvement initiatives will largely exist at secondary or tertiary areas of the company's organization.

Improvement initiatives develop as some grouping of technical projects and motivational techniques. However, without an articulated, integrated, and continuing general management focus, these programs cannot create fundamental improvement. In short, this is a major business downdraft for these companies.

BUSINESS PROBLEMS CAUSED BY LIMITED MANAGEMENT ATTENTION SPAN

Many companies that have experienced a major business downdraft make commitments to the various components of improvement, such as widespread training for organization learning and standardizing and normalizing basic financial and cost factors from receivables and centralized billing. Unfortunately, these commitments are often short-lived because company interests have turned elsewhere or technology has changed. This approach depends on a response to the currently squeakiest wheels or loudest voices among the company's business functions. Therefore, this form of improvement relies on a limited management attention span that sets in motion one project after another to deal with business problems, often under the umbrella of a business enhancement initiative that is highly promoted but has only a short time cycle.

Experience shows that this approach has difficulty in succeeding. That has been especially the case in organizations in which intermittently changing conditions have created variation in the effectiveness of strategy development, resource deployment, and processes and measurements. With wide imbalance and too little real integration and alignment of responsibility, each area marches to a different drumbeat within the company.

The hope that the incremental projects in themselves will bring about the necessary improvement is not likely to be realized in a company environment where strategy is difficult to implement. In such an environment plans are not always real and that makes everything else undependable: human resources planning, technology planning, training in improvement techniques, and the actual application of those techniques. It is like trying to massage one's toe without taking off one's shoe: One will never get to it.

The techniques driven by these projects—measurements, supplier cooperation, technology, statistical controls—are not likely to take permanent root. Moreover, these techniques are likely to require continual reinvention, under new names, with constant reemphasis as people are rotated, new action groups are established, and oxygen increasingly has to be pumped back into the initiative. After a few months of attempting some initiative or new technique, the employees of the organization—who have seen similar initiatives come and go—will ask what is different about this one compared with the several similar earlier initiatives that disappeared as somebody put his or her foot on the oxygen hose for that initiative. Genuine involvement and commitment disappear. The vulnerability of these companies is that they operate internally, in improvement terms, as a group of islands without bridges. That operational mode does not bring the full strength of the company to bear on improving the values of serving the customer.

Figure 10 shows how disconnected improvement planning and responsibilities result from this limited management attention span; it is based on data from organizations with these characteristics. Not surprisingly, the disconnected approach shows that improvements will "stick" far less frequently than will improvements that result from the quality of management that features excellence-driven leadership that builds on *connected* planning and *clarity* of responsibility.

Furthermore, there is a major contributing factor to this difference. Although these businesses carefully identify, measure, and track their performance results throughout their *physical* assets (i.e., from data-processing centers, production facilities, office equipment, and supplies), they are less likely to have established a similarly effective focus on their brand name, informational, and other *intangible* capacities. The organization may recognize that these intangibles are critically important to the effective implementation, operation, improvement, and alignment of these physical resources fully as much as they are to the overall business results. However, any relevant measurement in these organizations is likely to be confined to the traditional emphasis on the *expense budgets* for the staff whose work relates to these intangibles.

There is similarly wide variation among companies in terms of the extent to which they have developed their effective and efficient end-to-end systems and processes for directly integrating these "intangibles" with their physical assets within their management capital channels. This variation exists both in the degree to which they have a structured approach to the development of these systems and in a structured approach to the organization-aligned coordination of one system with another, recognizing their different purposes.

The disconnects represent a significant limitation of business growth in today's hugely competitive economic environment. At the same time, this presents a great opportunity for strong quality of management leadership. Examples of the disconnects can range from transactional services, from finance to insurance, and in manufacturing, as discussed in the next section of this chapter, and from organizations in health care to companies in hard and soft goods, which are discussed in the section after that.

Figure 10   Consistency of Improvement

"Disconnected" Improvement Development

EXECUTIVE
MANAGEMENT LEVELS
OPERATING LEVELS

Clarity of Responsibilities

Clear
Vague
Nonexistent

"Connected" Improvement Development

EXECUTIVE
MANAGEMENT LEVELS
OPERATING LEVELS

Clarity of Responsibilities

Vague
Clear

THE DIFFERENCES IN FREQUENCY OF IMPROVEMENT "STICKING"

```
            0                                              100
CONNECTED   [=====================================       ]
DISCONNECTED [======                                      ]
```

FREQUENCY OF IMPROVEMENT "STICKING"

DISCONNECTS FROM TRANSACTIONAL SERVICES TO MANUFACTURING

In some transactional services, such as finance and insurance, the emphasis on treasury capital investment and on information technology to improve efficiency and timing has been intense. The systems in these areas sometimes, however, have not been balanced or integrated with those directed toward customer satisfaction or with the requirements of the customers themselves. This nonintegration can increase the distance between the services organizations and their customers, especially as technology has changed. It can be a major limitation in their customer development and sales growth. Sometimes this limitation has not been immediately obvious to some management segments of these organizations, as compared to those of pacesetter service companies.

Similarly, in some manufacturing companies in which a very high proportion of operating costs goes to materials, a primary thrust of the business improvement emphasis has necessarily been on developing strong management systems with the *suppliers*. The focus has been for the vendor organizations to provide the company with significantly improved cost, delivery, and quality performance to help the company improve its operating results.

However, it is the company's *innovation* and product development *management* system and processes that specify the requirements that are critically important for suppliers to have as the guiding framework to achieve the goals of quality, costs and delivery. Because of the silo approach and the bureaucratic turf problems between the development processes and the supplier processes that continue in some companies, this systems integration does not take place productively, in contrast to the strong supply chain management systems that pacesetter companies have developed. Inevitably, the silo approach and turf wars extend the disconnects with suppliers, and this has limited the achievement of the intended benefits.

DISCONNECTS IN HEALTH CARE AND IN CONSUMER GOODS ORGANIZATIONS

The organization structure of some health care groups is likely to be in parallel segments. For example, administration, insurance, communications, and similar transactional activities are likely to be in one segment. Physician care, clinical practice, hospital service, and similar activities are likely to be in another, medical-oriented segment.

As health care has exploded in economic importance and management emphasis, the business and operating measurements in some health care organizations have grown in similarly parallel segments. For example, the administration segment may focus on inquiry response time, and the medical/clinical segment may focus on patient outcomes. However, several areas thread their way through both segments, thereby requiring integration and coordination of the relevant management operating systems. These areas, and these are just a few examples, include complete quality satisfaction, cost-effectiveness, response cycle times, and the information technology performance areas of critical importance to health care receivers and the organizations that are their financial providers.

In consumer goods organizations it is now standard practice for inventory and stocks to be precisely measured and tracked in terms of just-in-time, customer delivery cycle, and supply information technology. These measurements occur throughout the manufacturing, distribution, merchandising, and buyer purchase segments of the business flow. However, in some groups these measurements may not always be systematically time-integrated throughout these business segments.

As a result, in highly cyclic businesses—in spite of these islands of efficiency—there can remain problems with respect to production, product profitability, and quality satisfaction that can generate further problems related to *value, the customer,* and *overall company profitability.* Instead of becoming a productive sum for the company, this measurement and tracking primarily by segments can increasingly become a productive difference for some of these organizations.

By comparison, in pacesetter companies this measurement and tracking focus on clear, self-reinforcing systems and processes. These systems and processes are designed to sustain and grow sales and profitability throughout the procurement, marketing, distribution, financing, billing, collection, and customer quality satisfaction and retention chain. These companies are doing exactly that, with great competitive success.

RECONNECTING THE DISCONNECTS: FOCUSING THE PASSION, POPULISM, AND DISCIPLINED RESPONSIBILITY OF THE QUALITY OF LEADERSHIP

There is no misunderstanding about any of this in pacesetter companies that are successfully growing their sales and profitability in today's economic crucible. For example, the new chief executive officer (CEO) of a company—an highly experienced manager with strong and successful prior leadership in facing these issues—described the company's situation to his new associates after several weeks on the job had given him the opportunity to size up his and the company's challenges:

> The competitive strength of this organization's improvement initiatives after all the promotion over the recent past has gotten this company to the

five-yard line. The trouble is that it's our five-yard line—not the competitions'—and the competition continues to have the ball . . . I have never seen an organization with more well-documented business initiatives, improvement projects and programs—and less continuity of management commitment, attention, and implementation to them.

Companies today recognize that they can reap an enormous profitability and growth advantage by focusing on reconnecting these disconnects while simultaneously measuring and improving the productivity that results from this. That is the case because in this business era major business improvement means a better way to run the business, which then positions a company for a *further* better way to run the business. Continuous management improvement is a basic key to a company's ability to execute and implement in terms of the attitude that "we'll successfully manage our way as an organization in whatever business conditions there are." It's driven in pacesetter companies by the quality of management that is characterized by *passion, populism,* and *disciplined responsibility* (as discussed in detail in Chapter 3). These characteristics are fundamental to a company's ability to create and maintain the management capital attitude and emphasis that create and maintain its competitive strength:

- *Passion* relentlessly drives effective improvement through strong and consistent management of the organization's balanced and integrated actions.
- *Populism* emphasizes the human commitment and skill fundamental to making this happen.
- *Disciplined responsibility* provides the framework of end-to-end systems, processes, tools, resources, and strategies in and across the management capital channels that help and encourage each person in the organization (both individually and in teams) to think, act, and make decisions about how to provide superior performance. Disciplined responsibility also enables the company's leadership to implement the actions for serving customers and delivering consistently improving business results. It also provides the foundation for what we have come to think of as taking a business "physical" to find out how big and how fundamental the company's management innovation has to be to help employees throughout the company achieve the necessary improvement results.

THE DISCIPLINE IN ACTION: TAKING THE "BUSINESS PHYSICAL" TO DETERMINE HOW EXTENSIVE MANAGEMENT INNOVATION SHOULD BE IN OPPORTUNITY AREAS

Four management phases of this physical stand out:

1. Analysis
2. Planning
3. Construction
4. Measurement of effectiveness in terms of financial results and return on investment (ROI)

Each is discussed in the next sections.

ANALYSIS

The first phase is *analysis* through systematic patterns that fit the company. There are four goals in this phase of the physical:

- To rigorously identify the major business opportunities and issues in principal management capital channels that influence top-line growth and bottom-line profitability.
- To systematically investigate key questions in establishing this. Two of the key questions that are fundamental for many companies are the following:
  - How can we make our consumer customers more satisfied and more secure through effectiveness in these channels?
  - How can we make our industrial customers more competitive through effectiveness in these channels?
- To clearly establish both the physical and financial hard-asset elements as well as the soft-asset elements (e.g., technology, human resources, market and customer relationships, patents, and brands) that are the basis for performance in the channels.
- To determine the strengths (in terms of results in the management channel) and the weaknesses (in terms of disconnects, corresponding end-to-end systems demands, and business costs) that are keys to implementing this growth and performance.

For example, a manufacturing and services company applying this analysis established that its supply chain management channel was a major competitive business improvement area. Then it established the pattern of disconnects requiring action (see Figure 11). Finally, it established the corresponding system process deficiencies requiring action (see Figure 12), determining that only 40 percent of the original systems effectiveness was achieved on average across the system process components.

PLANNING FOR IMPROVEMENT

The second phase is planning through systematic approaches that fit the company. There are three goals for this phase of the physical:

- To rigorously establish the patterns reconnecting the disconnects and develop and improve the systems and processes that guide the full range of initiatives in the supply chain management channels. These processes are end-to-end, sequentially related, how-to-do action-based steps targeted toward specific performance results. The systems are the grouping of system process components that support the management channel results.
- To assure that this includes aggressively identifying and using global best practices, especially by emphasizing that what works well *anywhere*

Figure 11 Supply Chain Disconnects

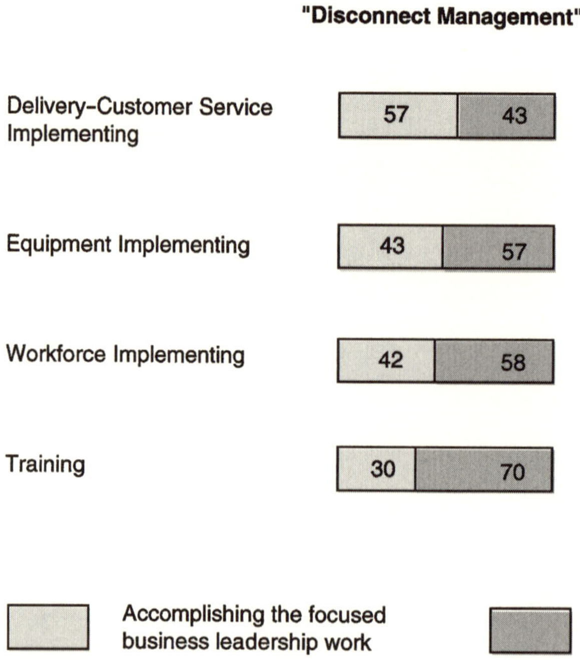

"Disconnect Management"

Delivery-Customer Service Implementing	57	43
Equipment Implementing	43	57
Workforce Implementing	42	58
Training	30	70

Accomplishing the focused business leadership work

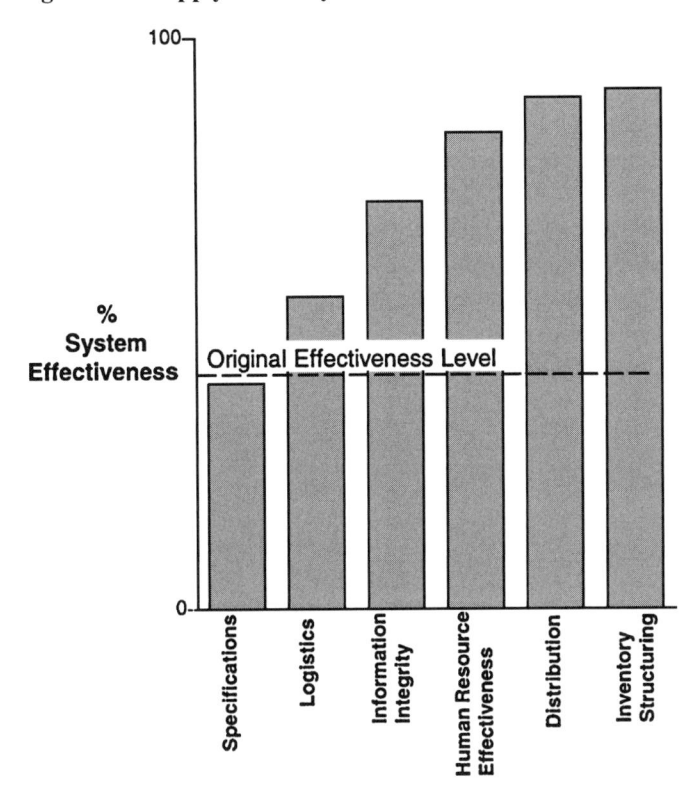

CHAPTER 6   SUSTAINING BUSINESS GROWTH BY RECOGNIZING AND RECONNECTING   109

Figure 12   Supply Chain Systems Effectiveness

[Bar chart showing % System Effectiveness across System Process Components: Specifications, Logistics, Information Integrity, Human Resource Effectiveness, Distribution, Inventory Structuring. A dashed horizontal line labeled "Original Effectiveness Level" crosses the bars, with bars increasing in height from left to right.]

SYSTEM PROCESS COMPONENTS

in the company is quickly available *everywhere* in the organization (where applicable).
- To accomplish this in ways that every involved person in the organization understands, believes in, and is part of.

CONSTRUCTION: RECONNECTING THE DISCONNECTS
The third phase is what is thought of as the "construction" or implementation of reconnecting these disconnects and establishing these systems and processes and other action steps throughout the supply chain management channel.

Figure 13 illustrates the company's improved results from what the company has described as "bolted-together management" in terms of reconnecting its disconnects (which were shown in Figure 11). Figure 14(*b*) illustrates the significant improvement in systems effectiveness to a level of more than 85 percent balanced throughout the supply chain management channel, as compared to the original effectiveness shown in Figure 14(*a*). Moreover, these results enormously increased the integrated management of tangible and intangible assets that were driving these supply management results.

FINANCIAL RESULTS AND ROI

Finally, the fourth phase is based on recognition that the measurement of effectiveness for management capital (as with financial capital) is financial results and ROI. Figure 15 shows the growth of the cash flow return from this quality-of-management discipline emphasis.

Figure 13 Bolted-Together Management: "Connecting the Disconnects Profitably"

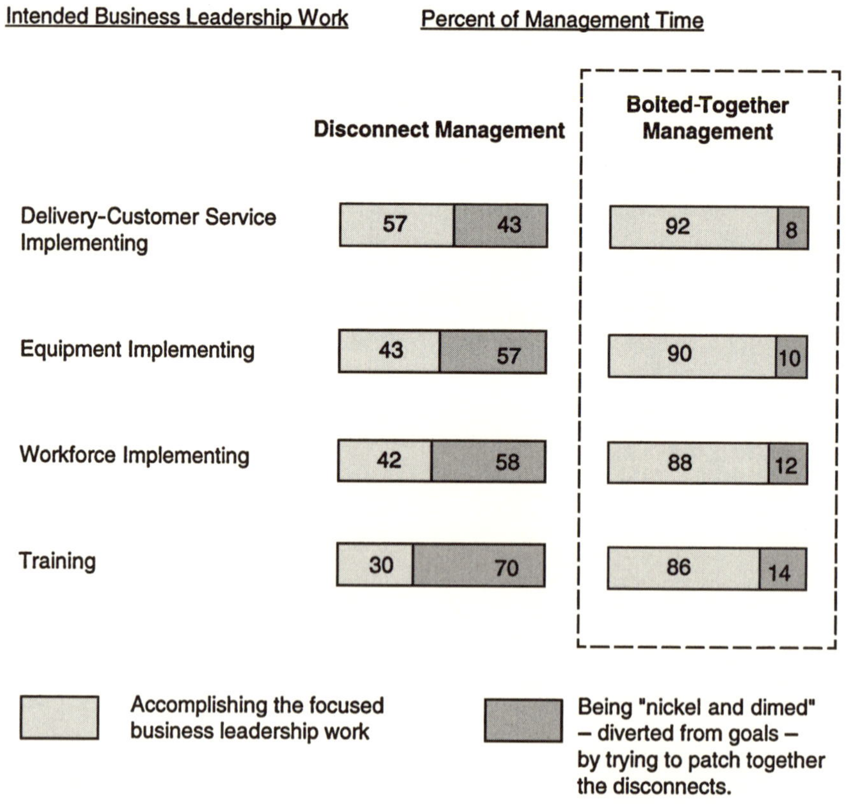

Intended Business Leadership Work | Percent of Management Time

	Disconnect Management	Bolted-Together Management
Delivery-Customer Service Implementing	57 / 43	92 / 8
Equipment Implementing	43 / 57	90 / 10
Workforce Implementing	42 / 58	88 / 12
Training	30 / 70	86 / 14

☐ Accomplishing the focused business leadership work

■ Being "nickel and dimed" — diverted from goals — by trying to patch together the disconnects.

Figure 14 *(a)* Supply Chain System Effectiveness

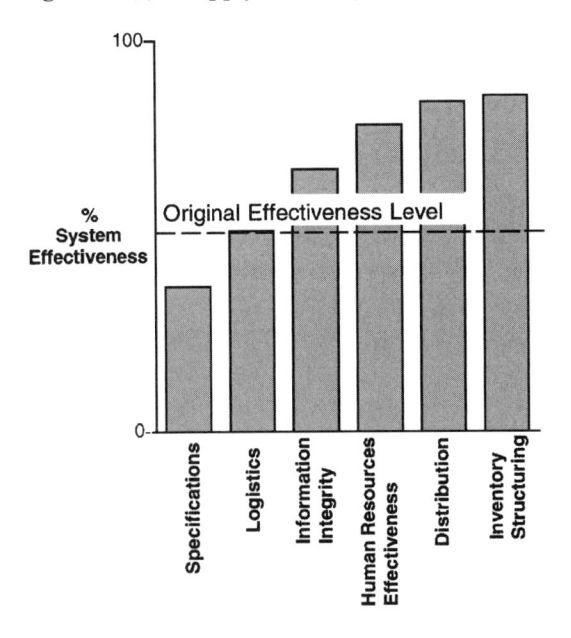

Figure 14 *(b)* Supply Chain System Effectiveness

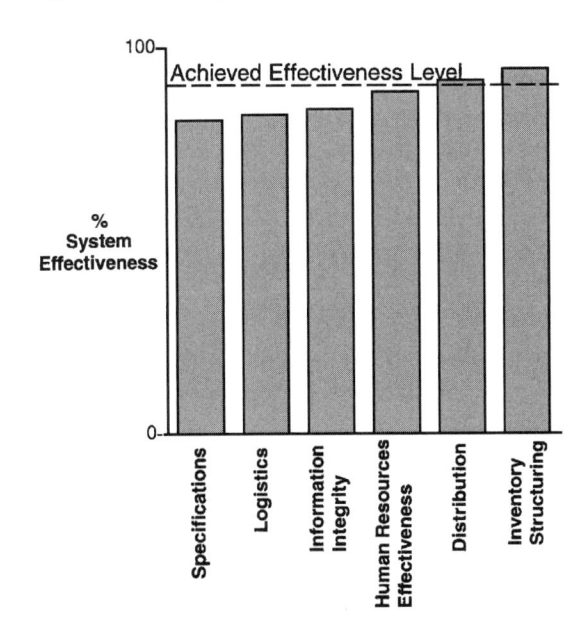

Figure 15 Supply Chain Cash Flow

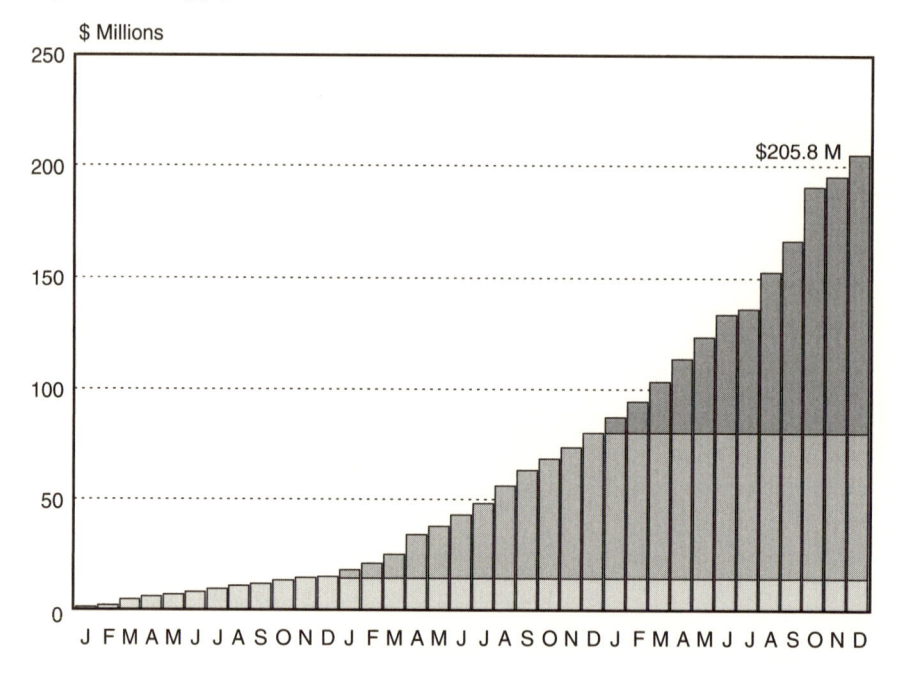

$205.8 M

CHAPTER 7

REDUCING FAILURE COSTS AND INCREASING SYSTEMS EFFECTIVENESS

A BASIC KEY to the pacesetter companies' creation of new business opportunity discussed in earlier chapters is the management capital–driven capability for rigorously increasing customer product and service value while simultaneously eliminating the business roadblocks that stand in its way. This capability differentiates pacesetters from companies in their marketplace that manage product development and operating improvement as separate initiatives with only a "best efforts" attitude (which has only mixed effectiveness) instead of adopting a fully committed character of integration among them.

The quality-of-management discipline removes the disconnects and the backward creep that make up the roadblocks. It measures them as business "failure" costs and lost opportunity costs in order to reduce and eliminate those costs.

This discipline is an important part of the leadership attitude of today's opportunistically driven company. It identifies for managerial guidance and planning the way in which a business's hard and soft assets contribute together to the total results of successful management innovation.

The importance of this discipline is amplified by the increasing speed with which today's business environment creates enormous changes in customer expectations, employee attitudes, technology shifts, international growth, and cost trends. Without these measurements and suitable planning to guide effective innovation, businesses that seem for a time to be doing well in pursuing their growth strategies and results can nonetheless—and for a while almost imperceptibly—become increasingly distanced from recognizing, evaluating, and improving the fundamental drivers of their business performance. This discipline must be managed systematically to keep backward creep from eroding the foundation for sustaining their growth.

Otherwise, this process becomes a fundamental, self-generated company management driver of a growth-decline-growth cycle. Some companies have spent the latter years of the twentieth century and the early years of the twenty-first century first trying to recover from this cycle and then trying to eliminate it. Some companies continue to remain highly vulnerable to this cycle.

THE BUSINESS RESULTS IMPACT OF DISCONNECTS: HIGH BUSINESS FAILURE COSTS AND LOST OPPORTUNITY COSTS

Leaders in today's opportunistically driven pacesetting companies recognize the management capital demand for relentless measurement and innovation.

They also realize that this demand must be met in advance—i.e., in the form of a preemptive strike—because of the potential for backward creep.

Otherwise, a substantial proportion of the productive capacity for sustaining profitable growth in these companies—for sales revenue creation, operations management, and cost-effectiveness—can be diminished by the disconnects and by the management capital deficiencies that are a primary cause of those disconnects. These disconnects and deficiencies are the primary drivers of the business failure costs and lost opportunity costs of those companies. Those costs are the economic quantification of losses and wasted resources resulting from the disconnects in satisfactorily completing required business tasks. The growth of such costs strongly affects the competitive and profitability performance of companies that after many years of cost *accounting* still sometimes have difficulty identifying what things really cost as a basis for strong cost *management*.

THE SCOPE OF BUSINESS FAILURE COSTS AND THEIR INTERNET TRANSPARENCY

These business failure and lost opportunity costs can progressively account for a substantial proportion of sales revenue in companies. These costs include many areas, including the following:

- The way a company ambiguously responds to a customer complaint—and so must respond again and again—together with the corresponding loss of sales and customer goodwill.
- An unclear focus with respect to new product or service development.
- Materials and products being lost and wasted because of distribution deficiencies.
- E-business glitches, which delay shipments to buyers because of process integration inadequacies in the company's Internet sales Web site. These inadequacies become immediately transparent to today's Web-savvy customer.

These deficiencies are primary embedded drivers of the so-called unproductive costs and high-overhead and fixed-cost burdens that hard-asset-oriented financial analysts and cost accountants identify; unfortunately, too frequently those financial analysts and cost accountants have been unable to identify the *root cause* of those costs. The *reason* for the cost is what is needed for twenty-first-century companies to first understand how to reduce these costs and then to take action to achieve that goal.

STRUCTURING BUSINESS FAILURE COSTS AND CREATING OPPORTUNITIES

As was mentioned at the beginning of this chapter, a key management capital objective is to integrate the increase in product and service value with the removal of the roadblocks to achieving that goal. A frequently used metric for focusing upon business failure cost is to measure the quality costs of delivering complete customer satisfaction with the company's products and services as a percentage of sales revenue.

Our experience and data indicate that business failure costs focused in these quality cost terms can amount to 20 percent or more of sales revenue in many companies compared with only 5 to 10 percent and less of sales revenue in pacesetter companies: Their management capital capacity for constantly effective innovation helps those companies reduce and eliminate the disconnects and backward creep that generate these costs. At the same time the reduction and elimination correspondingly create the resulting business opportunities, with their potential for generating new profit growth.

Major companies employ these measurements as key business guideposts. They recognize them as key business indicators. At Union Pacific Railroad, one of the oldest and continuingly successful large American companies and one of the most widely recognized American brand names, the CEO, Dick Davidson, and his associates have reported on their results during regular quarterly business meetings.

Costs measured in these terms have four components:

1. *External failure costs.* These include costs generated *in the marketplace* by the unsatisfactory performance of products and services and the unsatisfactory completion of business tasks required for delivering *complete* customer quality satisfaction.
2. *Internal failure costs.* These include costs generated *within the company network* by this unsatisfactory performance of products and services and the unsatisfactorily completed business tasks required for delivering complete customer quality satisfaction.
3. *Appraisal.* These include costs associated with key systems, processes, and Internet functions that provide controls to ensure complete customer satisfaction.

4. *Prevention.* These include costs associated with initiatives for forestalling the disconnects and backward creep that can affect complete customer satisfaction.

Figure 16 diagrams this structure. Because of differences in markets, products and services, organizations, geographic scope, and other considerations, each company must define the specific measurement areas within these components that best fit its own business requirements. Figure 17 shows two of the examples—one from manufacturing and one from banking/finance.

The importance of this measurement becomes clearer when leaders and managers recognize that failure costs measured in these terms are an indicator of what might be termed a company's "hidden organization." For example, analyzing failure costs can reveal the following:

- Disconnects that affect customer satisfaction, innovation, time cycle compression and global expansion and thus limit potential growth in sales revenues.

Figure 16   Business Failure Cost Structure

CHAPTER 7 REDUCING FAILURE COSTS AND INCREASING SYSTEMS EFFECTIVENESS   119

Figure 17 Business Failure Cost Measurements in Manufacturing and in Banking and Finance

MANUFACTURING

External Failure
- Product or Service Liability
- Warranty
- Policy Adjustments

Internal Failure
- Scrap — Internal
- Rework– Internal
- Scrap and Rework Related to Vendor
- Excess Labor and Materials
- Failure Investigation and Correction
- Product and Process Redesign
- Downtime and Delays

Appraisal
- Test and Inspection of Purchased Material
- Measuring Services
- Field Testing
- Approval Expenditures
- Process or Product Evaluation and Report
- Quality Information Equipment Expense
- Quality Audits

Prevention
- Quality and Reliability Analysis and Planning
- Quality Training and Manpower Development
- Specification, Design, and Development of Quality Information Equipment

TYPICAL BUSINESS FAILURE COSTS IN BANKING AND FINANCE

External Failure
- Lost Business
- Writeoffs
- Customer Attrition
- Customer Complaints
- Fraud
- Legal/Regulatory Failure
- Collections
- Resolving Customer Disputes
- Statement Errors
- NCL

Internal Failure
- Computer Downtime
- Nonperforming Assets
- Defective Purchased Material and Services
- Data Entry Errors
- Hedging Errors
- Rework
- Employee Turnover

- Erosion of growth capacities as a result of the use of these capacities in responding to business failures, thus requiring further hard- and soft-asset investment for increased product or service volumes.
- Ineffective use of resources because of a lack of integration in leveraging improvements achieved throughout the organization. Integration often is not achieved because the organization lacks systematic processes for assuring that what works well *anywhere* in the organization is given consideration *everywhere* in the organization. Some organizations also fail to develop effective processes for benchmarking or obtaining competitive intelligence about other companies in order to implement improvements discovered at those companies. All these failures contribute to lost sales revenues as well as significant excess operating costs.

Figure 18 reflects the principle of the effect in high-disconnect companies on the corporate capacity of the hidden organization defined by these business failure costs and the degree of the improvement required for restoring this lost capacity to achieve productive results.

MANAGING FAILURE COSTS AS KEY IN BUSINESS STRATEGY IN ALL MARKET CONDITIONS

All this illustrates the central role that management of business failure costs can play in the leadership attitude of managing in all business conditions to sustain and accelerate business growth and profitability. Of course, strong markets help, but economic conditions may not consistently provide support from that source.

At Tenneco, in spite of the strength of the company's products and businesses, its successive CEOs Mike Walsh and Dana Mead could not count on market growth in a difficult economy. They also could not count on what Mead described as "technological silver bullets." Moreover, price relief was stymied by excess industry capacity. However, as Mead reported, they *could* control how *efficiently* they worked. Therefore, Dana Mead continued to focus Tenneco strongly—and effectively—on managing its systematic measurement and reduction of business failure costs as a key to improving efficiency.

The result was the elimination of more than $2 billion in failure costs from their businesses and the addition of nearly $1 billion over time to Ten-

CHAPTER 7   REDUCING FAILURE COSTS AND INCREASING SYSTEMS EFFECTIVENESS   121

Figure 18   Business Failure Cost Measures of a Hidden Organization and the Improvement Requirement for Restoring Productive Growth

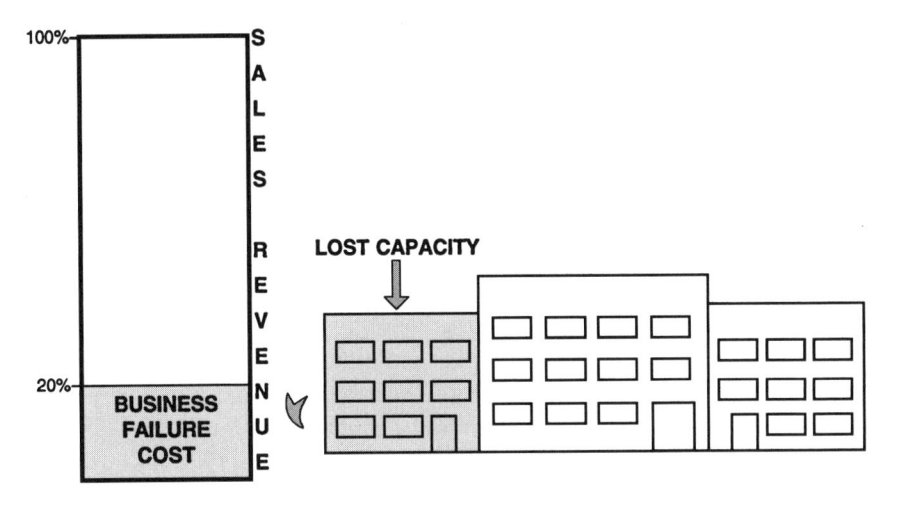

BUSINESS FAILURE COST TRANSLATES INTO A HIDDEN ORGANIZATION

neco's operating income as Tenneco and General Systems worked together. Those changes were a key factor in increasing customer and product service value while eliminating business roadblocks and the disconnects that create them. Correspondingly, they were a key factor in increasing the strength and value of Tenneco's businesses.[1]

BUSINESS FAILURE COST MANAGEMENT: HARDWARE AND SOFTWARE INFORMATION SYSTEMS

An example of business failure cost management is the performance of an organization whose businesses focus on the development, production, and marketing of software and hardware information systems together with services to install and implement them. Those businesses continually

---

[1] From Dana G. Mead with Thomas C. Hayes, *High Standards, High Choices*, New York, Wiley, 2000.

faced major cycles of substantial increase in business volume, followed by flat periods or significant downturns and then by upturns. These dramatic business cycles had a major effect on the company's profitability and growth.

An important factor in this cycle was the pricing of the company's products in the face of periodic sharp price reductions by competitors. The company was generally strong in price maintenance when its products were first in the market and it could maintain a strong pricing policy. However, when its products became commoditized (as had increasingly become the case) the company's cost structure was too high and too inflexible to be effectively responsive to price competition. This problem was far more intense when the company entered markets with those of its products which had good customer value but were not first in the market.

These variable cycles in growth and profitability were therefore not by any means entirely market-driven; in fact, the company's markets were continuing to grow. Nor were these cycles created by any weakness in the company's technological strength, which was high. Instead, they were caused by competitive weakness in the integration of the company's product, production, and marketing effectiveness in the face of strong competitors and demanding customers.

As a key component of its major initiative to improve this effectiveness, the company turned to the metrics of business failure cost management and focused on certain leadership areas to help identify and deal with the relevant business factors that could establish and drive improvement.

The company's failure analysis revealed performance disconnects in its product development, manufacturing, and marketing. As the data were quantified in economic terms, they showed clearly that *the company's aggregate business failure cost amounted to 23 percent of sales revenue,* which represented an enormous diversion of the company's economic capacity. Approximately 50 percent of this was in internal failure costs, 25 percent in external failure, 20 percent in appraisal costs; and only 5 percent in prevention costs, as is shown in Figure 19.

Those metrics indicated that one of the principal issues was the significant diversion of critically necessary new product development resources that were consistently pulled off to deal with problems in supply, production, and marketing. Moreover, that draining off of development resources consistently delayed or reduced new product releases. A further resource drain was created by the demand for development resources in resolving customer problems in newly launched products in the field.

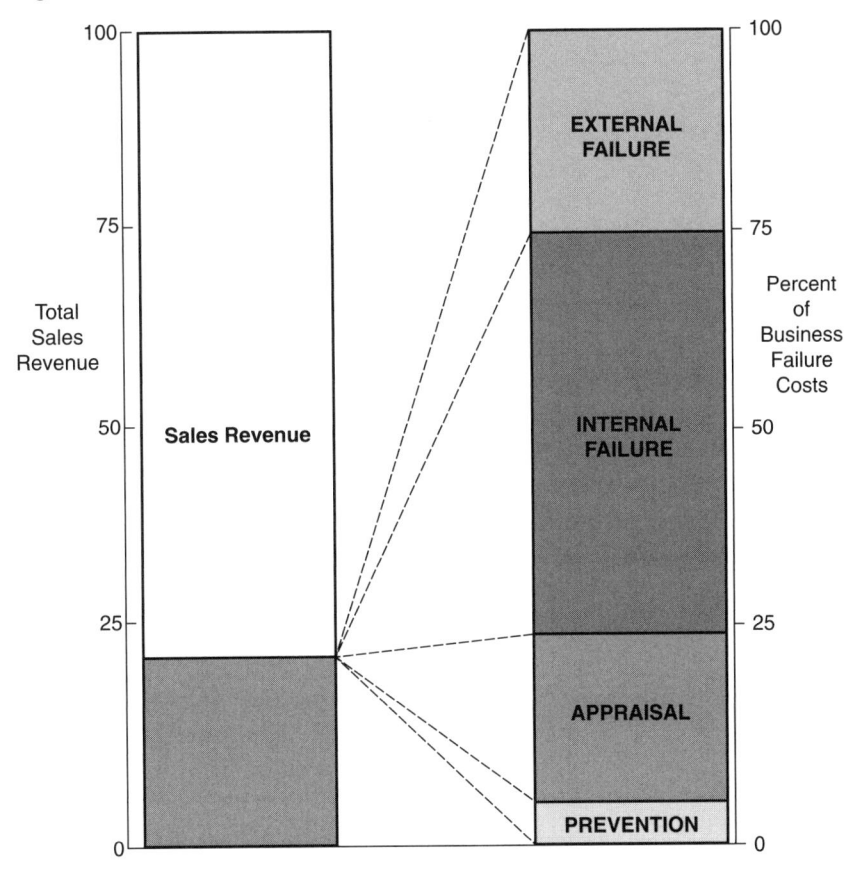

CHAPTER 7   REDUCING FAILURE COSTS AND INCREASING SYSTEMS EFFECTIVENESS   **123**

Figure 19   Business Failure Cost as a Percent of Sales

Total Sales Revenue / Sales Revenue

Percent of Business Failure Costs: EXTERNAL FAILURE, INTERNAL FAILURE, APPRAISAL, PREVENTION

These disconnects generally had been widely recognized and discussed in the company, but recognition and discussion were not enough; the problem was deeper than that:

- The full magnitude of the disconnects had not been quantified.
- The causes of the disconnects had not been fully identified in fact-based terms.
- The limitations they created in both customer value and competitive positioning had not been defined.
- The leadership and management actions for networking the improvement actions had not been established.

Systematic analysis of the failure costs made clear and identified the large number of disconnects in technical, informational, training, and other areas that were creating these problems throughout the business's development, supply, production, marketing, distribution, and Internet cross-functional actions. Among other things, it indicated the glitches taking place because of periodic development and sales emphasis in *individual* hardware or software product terms rather than in terms of *complete* customer solutions.

Systematic analysis also focused attention on both the high *external* as well as *internal* failure costs that were being generated by the backward creep from the performance objectives that were established. The company was too slow in leading or at least responding to rapid changes in customer and quality expectations throughout the business's markets.

The initiatives designed for the consequent improvements were directed toward significant management innovation in prevention actions focused on those disconnects. To support those targeted innovation actions, the company more than doubled its prevention cost investment. The initiatives were structured to provide far more effective leadership and management that would focus on step-by-step systematic strengthening of the *integration* of development processes throughout the company's supply, production, and distribution chain. Those prevention initiatives also focused major innovational attention on developing, understanding, and staying ahead of customer requirements and quality expectations. Figure 20 illustrates some representative components of the resulting integrated system network.

Throughout the subsequent 12- to 24-month period, this innovation action relentlessly focused on those business demands. Gradually, the company eliminated most of the cyclic effects that had critically affected its results, and that change was reflected in significant improvements in the company's performance and profitability—and in the consistency of those results. Moreover, the combination of a far more focused and faster product and service development with the stronger cost structure was demonstrated in much stronger pricing strength.

All this was indicated in the savings from the over 50 percent reduction in business failure costs that was used to measure those improvements. Figure 21 illustrates this economics of business failure cost management as a primary measurement and improvement driver of these business results; it also shows the additional capacity for improvement profitability and growth that is the counterpart of these results.

Figure 20 Some Representative Components of an Integrated System Network

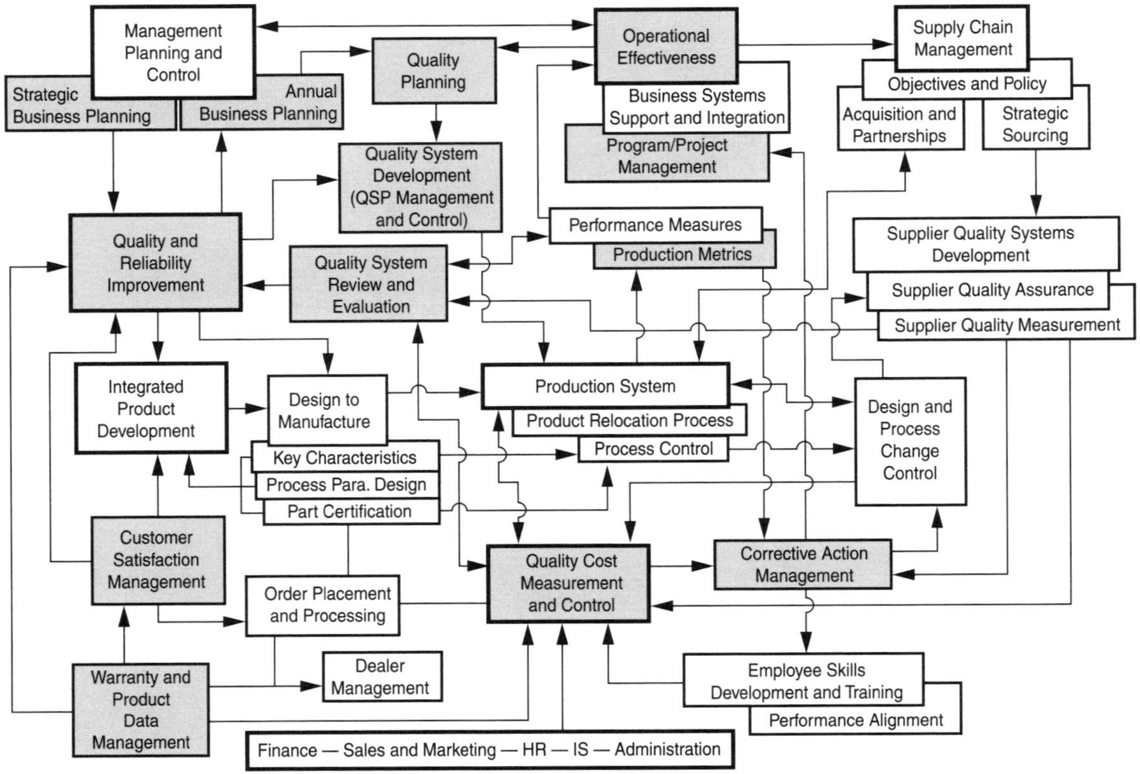

125

THE STRENGTH OF SYSTEMS EFFECTIVENESS VERSUS HUMAN BRIDGES

A principal cause of the improved business results discussed in the previous example was the focused effectiveness of company *leadership*. However, some companies, by comparison, find that their capacity for creating customer and product service value—and their capacity for eliminating business roadblocks—generates a mixture of actions. Correspondingly, those actions vary widely in terms of how effective and how well-integrated they are unless *the leadership emphasis* is effectively articulated, measured, and implemented.

By comparison, the competitive strength of pacesetter companies derives from their capacities specifically to *connect* increased customer value with roadblock removal. Those capacities are strategized and planned, and then they are networked and diffused throughout the organization, with a systems and process effectiveness that becomes a huge competitive advantage. This helps and encourages every person in the organization—both individually and in teams—to rapidly and consistently think, act, decide on, and integrate solutions that provide superior performance results. This system provides the tools and training to accomplish this goal.

This emphasis makes these actions a multiplying sum for those organizations. It is not the dividing difference that is created in other companies that are led and managed with an uncertain mixture of systematic actions together with much slower case-by-case, situation-by-situation actions.

In these latter companies, such actions may be decided by best efforts communications and negotiations across the "human bridges" over which departmental communications and actions travel but without focused processes and criteria guided by clear leadership emphasis and measurements. Without clear measurement and reduction of these disconnects, particularly in companies facing tough market and business conditions, the following problems can arise:

- Product and service development can be both too slow and too costly.
- Information management can be a group of technology, data-processing, and administrative silos without fully effective support for business decision making and e-business.
- Improvement initiatives and cost reductions can overlook or eliminate strong and highly productive activities together with unproduc-

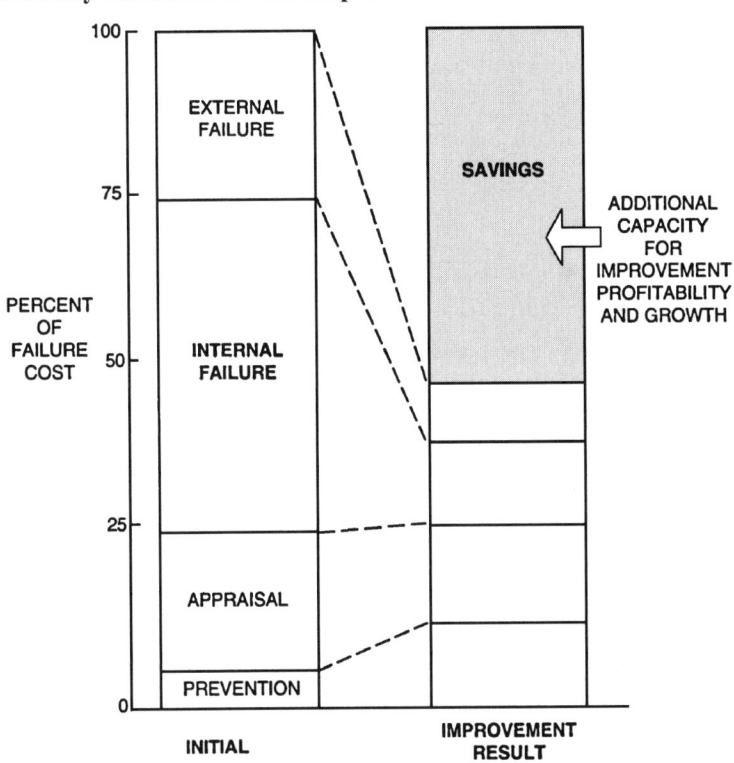

CHAPTER 7 REDUCING FAILURE COSTS AND INCREASING SYSTEMS EFFECTIVENESS   127

Figure 21 Economics of Business Failure Cost Management as a Primary Measurement and Improvement Driver

**TARGETED MANAGEMENT INNOVATION INVESTMENT
TO REDUCE IDENTIFIED FAILURES FOR
IMPROVED GROWTH AND PROFITABILITY**

tive ones, never really getting to the basic causes of these failure costs.

The resulting difference in business performance created in these terms among companies can be enormous. Our data show that for some companies process and systems effectiveness can be 35 to 40 percent, as in the initial performance of the supply chain management examples described in Chapter 6. This is in comparison to 85 percent or more as in the improved result achieved in that supply chain example. Figure 22 identifies some of the differences in the organizational character of this system impact on thinking, learning, acting, and deciding, which are critical to sustaining and accelerating company profitability and growth.

It often is said that knowledge is strength, but business experience shows that knowledge becomes and remains strength only through *leadership with the management capital attitude*. This attitude maintains that this systematic learning organization emphasis is one of the keys to a company's character and culture for sustaining and extending profitable growth.

Figure 22   Organizational Character of System Impact on Thinking, Learning, Acting, and Deciding

	30% – 40% Effective	**80% – 90% Effective**
Senior Management	System "cheerleader"	System implementation leader, developer of the management system "playbook"
Business Focus	Defined in company terms	Company results focused in customer terms
System Actions	Fireworks displays of incremental improvement Episodic motivation sessions Hip-shooting many individual techniques No integrated management framework Doesn't stick, and people know it	Relentless long-term detailed system implementation and continuous improvement Rigorous system process methodology
Output Approach	Make product and offer services quicker and cheaper, sell hard, finance cleverly	Making product with higher customer value means quicker and cheaper
System Training	Intermittent Not job-related Off-line involvement program	Continuous learning Scheduled and in line with total program Tools and techniques taught integral with system for their use
Recognition and Reward	Recognition of value improvement periodically Not reward factor	Improvement major reward factor
Leadership Concept	Get ideas out of boss's head into workers hands Promotion means make the boss happy	Empower the knowledge, skills and attitude of people Promotion means make the customer happy and that makes a smart boss happy
Middle Management	Minimal time on integrated system improvement	Significant time on systems management and empowerment

CONSTANT MANAGEMENT INNOVATIONS THAT REDUCE PRODUCT AND SERVICE CYCLES AND DEVELOPMENT COSTS

One of the key areas characterizing this management capital attitude and emphasis is the relentless *management* innovation—not only technology innovation—throughout the product and service development and introduction management channel in pacesetter companies. It provides one of the primary competitive advantage opportunity areas in today's markets. This advantage lies in implementing new technology in terms of both of the following:

- Developing customer value–creating products and services
- Reducing cycle time and cost throughout the business value–creating chain of supply, production, and distribution management, to which technology must connect but often does not

The urgency of this management innovation is driven by how rapidly new products are being matched or made quickly obsolete by new competitive offerings in today's markets. This speed necessitates further intense urgency to constantly reduce product development and launch cycles. This urgency is further driven by the pressures derived from the way the costs of development launch, distribution, and maintenance have become a major factor in the economy of profitability.

AN EXAMPLE: MANAGEMENT INNOVATION AT AN AUTOMOTIVE MANUFACTURING COMPANY

An example is the product development and production areas of a multicomponent mechanical product manufacturing organization with a relentless management capital attitude and an emphasis on generating constant management innovation for accomplishing this necessary improvement in systems effectiveness. The focus has been on progressively developing and installing successive innovations in product planning, development, and manufacturing engineering.

Figure 23 shows both the system process components that have been powering these management innovations and their results. Significant attention has been placed on the following areas:

- The knowledge creation and utilization foundation for establishing measurement milestone criteria for management review and control of resource commitments
- Integration of design verification and production validation testing
- Structured sharing of concurrent program experience

This emphasizes design management effectiveness with direct customer connections, including the development and integration of new computer design, production, and process state-of-the-art simulation for statistically establishing product and process parameters. It greatly reduces the costly, time-consuming, and sometimes inaccurate steps of always "going to metal" in establishing and testing these part and product features as a condition for design and manufacturing process decisions.

Together with progress throughout several other system process components, this design management improvement has generated major cycle

Figure 23 Reducing Product Development Cycles and Launch Time and Costs

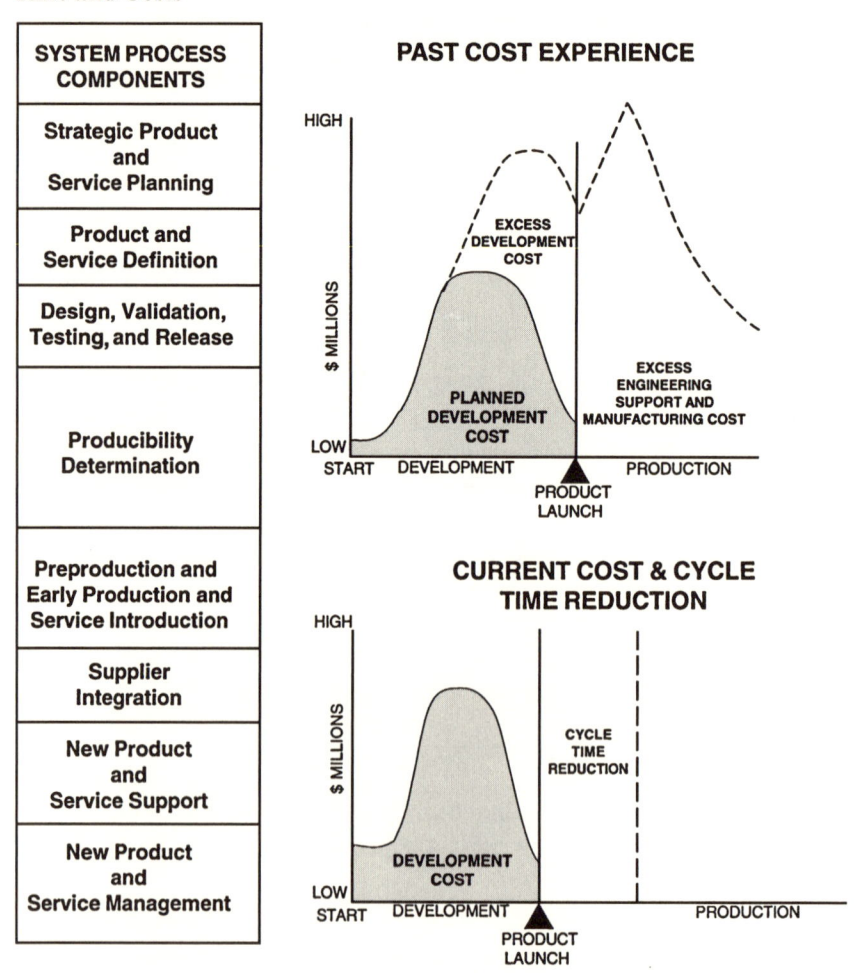

SYSTEM PROCESS COMPONENTS
Strategic Product and Service Planning
Product and Service Definition
Design, Validation, Testing, and Release
Producibility Determination
Preproduction and Early Production and Service Introduction
Supplier Integration
New Product and Service Support
New Product and Service Management

and development cost reductions. For example, it has eliminated one prototype series out of three because of improved planning and integration of customer requirements for "workhorse" hardware for the initial development of the prototype. This design management improvement has reduced total test time and resources by consolidating the development validation and production validation test requirements and data. This design management improvement has produced more effective management of resource commitments across stages of development through the milestone review requirement on an international basis. Taken together, all this has provided great competitive advantage for the company in one of the world's most demanding marketplaces.

In addition, these management innovations have achieved the following outstanding improvements:

- Reduced development cycle time by more than 50 percent
- Increased research and development (R&D) productivity 250 percent
- Effectively implemented global integration of development milestone reviews throughout all international units of the organization

As shown in Figure 23, excess development cost has been significantly lowered and cycle time has been dramatically reduced. This has increased the company's competitive strength for growth and profitability.

AN EXAMPLE: INCREASING SYSTEMS EFFECTIVENESS AT A HEALTH CARE FACILITY

A large medical center's initiative to significantly improve health care delivery provides an example of major results in an entirely different institutional and organizational context. This medical center adopted a management capital emphasis on fundamental innovation for providing improved systems effectiveness. The medical center's objective was directed toward three primary areas:

- Improving patient care
- Reducing the costs of its delivery
- Increasing the growth of revenues

The emphasis was on key delivery capability areas that were basic to those results. Among the recognized key opportunities were its hospital bed capacity, its nursing resource utilization, and its operating room throughput. These opportunities provided the leverage for improvements throughout the medical center.

Particular consideration was given to the new character required in the initiatives for meeting the demand for major improvement results in such capabilities. In the past the medical center had been able to effect partial improvement solutions, but those solutions were limited by interfunctional blocks. Those blocks were characterized by disconnects created by the organizational schism that periodically developed, which was not atypical of medical center operations. The major problems were created by differences in attitude, human resource training and background, financial patterns; and sometimes objectives that could divide the medical center's finance, billing, and other administrative areas from the medical center's clinical areas.

The medical center's management leadership changed this schism by clearly emphasizing a new and overarching central theme for focusing on meeting the huge challenges faced by health care deliverers. The medical center also emphasized the character of the actions needed to meet those challenges. It initiated a new orientation toward genuinely coordinated actions for improvement throughout the medical center's organization.

Careful attention was paid to team-based relationship patterns that began with the systematic, fully integrated analysis of the key capabilities that had long been recognized as the leverage for organizationwide improvement. Among the integrating metrics used was the cost of delivering complete satisfaction (in this case patient satisfaction rather than traditional customer/consumer satisfaction) to further identify and make visible areas of needed investments for required change.

The medical center conducted step-by-step planning and implementation of improvement actions to develop systematic integration and processes. Then it established steps and metrics for coordinated improvement actions, with widespread participation from throughout the medical center community. The ensuing actions generated the following results in terms of improvements in patient care and service availability:

- More effective nursing resource application, assisted by what the chief nursing officer summarized as "the management processes needed to get all the medical areas to manage their resources the same way"
- Significant improvement in hospital bed utilization
- Much better operating room capability for serving patients by improving turnaround capacity
- Greatly increased ability to serve patients from affiliated health centers

- Major reduction in the required overtime hours for accomplishing key tasks

All these improved results, together with many other improvements, greatly helped the medical center move forward in achieving its objectives of improving patient care, reducing costs, and increasing revenues.

THE QUALITY-OF-MANAGEMENT DISCIPLINE THAT INTEGRATES THE GROWTH OF A COMPANY'S *SALES* WITH THE GROWTH OF ITS *EFFECTIVENESS*

The results in the range of examples that have been discussed in this chapter span very different products, services, and markets. What the examples have in common is the *management capital leadership capability* for rigorously increasing customer product and service value while simultaneously eliminating roadblocks that stand in the way. This leadership capability provides a major strength in today's heavily competitive economic environment. Measuring the disconnects as business failure costs and lost opportunity costs—and integrating their continuous improvement through a rigorous increase in systems effectiveness—is a central part of the leadership attitude of today's opportunistically driven pacesetting companies.

Such leadership provides the basis for a company's simultaneous direct management focus on the business's *sales and revenue growth* together with the business's *effectiveness growth*. Those factors are "joined at the hip" managerially from the top to the bottom of the company, and this integration is the key to maintaining and accelerating the company's profitability.

This is a fundamentally different approach from that of some companies, where this essential coupling of running the business to grow and improving the business's effectiveness has been managed in separate organization silos without effective alignment, coordinated priorities, organizational or long-term managerial or leadership attention spans, comparable systematic discipline, or comparable growth in sales and profitability.

CHAPTER 8

DEVELOPING VISIBLE AND INVISIBLE COMPETITIVE STRENGTH AND "MATERIALIZING" MANAGEMENT CAPITAL

A FACTOR IN BUSINESS EXPERIENCE that threaded its way through the previous chapters is how judgment and intellect have increasingly become the powerhouse of business and organizational results when they are effectively led, inspired, managed, networked, and diffused by means of the empowerment of end-to-end systems and processes in key management capital channels.

This management approach is critical regardless of whether a company is selling a turbine, transportation, foodstuffs, diesel engines, a shirt, a memory chip, automotive products, credit cards, a computer, pharmaceuticals, software, broadband communications, or a personal service. Fundamental to what the company is really developing, producing, and marketing is the *intellectual content*, the human resources-motivated *competence*, and the other *soft-asset capabilities* that go into these products and services fully as much as do the silicon, steel, pharmacopeia, brick and mortar, and equipment that are used to develop, produce, and market those products and services.

Companies must manage these capabilities effectively in order to provide the value of a completely satisfactory customer experience that will develop loyalty and repeat business. How effectively a company manages these capabilities is what determines its ability to make the large and small moves that now drive competitive leadership. Today's pacesetting leaders recognize the importance of accomplishing this successfully because they see the harsh business reality that the competitive forces throughout the world will make the economic demands of the recent past look like merely a warm-up for the brutal business requirements that will dominate the next several years.

BUSINESS CHARACTERISTICS THAT DRIVE SUCCESS IN PACESETTING COMPANIES

Four primary business characteristics stand out in the management capital attitude and emphasis of companies that are accomplishing this successfully:

1. Understanding, respecting, and responding to customers is critical.
2. Being a leader requires the extension of leadership throughout the organization.
3. The way a company works should be continuously improving, and customers should be informed of the improvements.

4. Continuous improvement requires specific objectives, with a timetable, structure, and support to meet those objectives and with excellence in their implementation and execution.

This chapter begins by discussing each of these characteristics in detail.

1. UNDERSTANDING, RESPECTING, AND RESPONDING TO CUSTOMERS

The first characteristic of pacesetter companies is their understanding of, respect for, and responsiveness to today's very well-informed and extremely demanding global customer. These companies emphasize leadership that responds to the fundamental shift in customer expectations that has been driven by the enormous explosion of demand for greater purchase value throughout the world. In consumer marketplaces this shift is powered by a combination of the growing consumption demands in the face of pressures on wage earners' family income (particularly in mature market areas) and a volcanic upsurge for elevating standards of life (especially in emerging market areas). In these market areas of the world the principle that "families cannot afford to buy cheap—only good" is everywhere, from the schools to the workplace.

For business buyers the shift is driven by the economic pressures of the last few years. Those pressures have led to a demand for the reliable, predictable operation of equipment and services purchased, with no necessary provision for costly equipment backup and little tolerance for the time or cost of any failures.

Businesses that serve these markets with products and services on these terms are the companies structured for accelerating their sales revenue growth. Businesses can no longer rely on the kind of marketing positioning that evolved for the sales concepts of an earlier, less demanding day. Pacesetter companies understand that there is no substitute for direct contact with their customers in the forms that best fit the situation. They also recognize that unless it is made a rigorous discipline in itself, such direct contact can be very difficult to do in light of today's time demand pressures.

It can be easy enough to be involved with the customer on paper, through market research, and through the increasing effectiveness of customer-focused technology. It can be an entirely different matter to look a customer in the eye and say: "I really want you to tell me what you think." The response can be traumatic, but it is essential.

For example, consider the new chief executive of a major company whose initial emphasis was on shaping the company with strong customer connection and responsiveness. The CEO received many reports about the extensive use and proven value of new technology that could provide information about customers. However, he raised one principal question with each of the many managers with whom he met face to face on his first overview visits throughout the company's various facilities. He asked them, "In the last six months how many of you have personally sat with your major and as many as possible of your smaller customers and asked about your products and services?"

He reported on the answer to this question in remarks to his first companywide conference with all the managers and executives. Only about one of three key managers was able to answer his question satisfactorily in terms that fit the business circumstances. This result has since been greatly improved, with a correspondingly increased pattern of far more favorable customer relations as the company has accelerated its sales growth and revenue.

2. BEING A LEADER REQUIRES EXTENDING LEADERSHIP

The second characteristic of pacesetter companies is their emphasis on the idea that business leadership must be extended systematically and rigorously. There has always been a lot of debate, of course, about whether this quarter-to-quarter heat one lives with in the corporate kitchen is a good thing in the long term. But pacesetter companies seem to thrive on this heat while placing great emphasis on prudent, effective, open, responsible action and disclosure that take into account the business realities that exist during economic fluctuations and up-and-down cycles.

Of course, there is in fact very little choice about attention to short- and long-term performance for two very practical reasons. The first obvious reason is simply that customers, investors and everyone else focus on both. The other reason for company management is that the single toughest management job is to build forward momentum in an organization. But once a company lets it slip and takes a breather for a while, it may never get that full momentum back. Furthermore, losing momentum also creates disastrous internal problems because when a company is up, members of the winning team battle with the competition, but when it is down, members of the team that has stopped winning battle with *each other*.

3. CONCENTRATE ON BEING BETTER AND GETTING CREDIT FOR IT

The third characteristic of pacesetter companies is that they use consistent improvement to sell their companies as strongly as they sell their products and services—and they promote this fact aggressively to their customers. They concentrate both on being better and on getting credit for it. Market studies show that when customers size up products—whether they are Cummins Diesel Engines or Intel chips—what they perceive is not only the product but also *what they have read and heard* favorably about the company's highly committed executives and workforce, the company's belief in its own customer service, and just plain confidence that the company is good and is getting even better—i.e., the company's reputation.

4. SPECIFIC OBJECTIVES, TIMETABLE, STRUCTURE, SUPPORT, IMPLEMENTATION, AND EXECUTION

The fourth characteristic is that improvement requires very specific objectives, with a timetable, structure, and support to meet those objectives. Pacesetter companies recognize that the organization's culture for improvement is far more than a philosophy supported by incremental improvement. Success requires a culture for improvement far better than that of many companies whose approach has been incremental improvement, which is characterized by one project after another, under some form of an "improvement umbrella," which employees, based on past experience, may recognize as temporary. This approach does not work, especially if similar initiatives in the past have died after a short life cycle and been buried without an autopsy. This approach is problematic because people change jobs, new task forces are always being formed, and this kind of improvement structure just ends up being jerry-rigged.

Instead, the key characteristic of this fourth characteristic is its focus on the development and deployment of the company's management capital to assure the business's leadership in two fundamental ways to compete, which are the keys to business performance. In addition, these two ways should be well integrated to ensure successful competition.

TWO FUNDAMENTAL WAYS TO COMPETE: "VISIBLE" VALUE CREATION

The first way to compete is to effectively and efficiently lead the "visible" value creation competitive strength of the company. This involves managing in terms of the competition between *the company's* products and services and *its competitors'* products and services, whether steel, plastic, silicon, software, financial transactions, health care outcome, or product delivery. This effectiveness and efficiency is measured by sales and market scorecard criteria concerning whether customers judge that the company's offerings are better and whether the company is good at helping them buy accordingly. These criteria are widely recognized, universally available, and often rigorously benchmarked. This approach to competition is what has largely been meant, measured, and taught as "competitive leadership" since the days of Adam Smith.

Management leadership of value-creating visible competition is a basic condition for business success. It is about the products and services that customers see in the company. It tracks the direct source of the company's revenues. It is the in-line operation of running the business to generate these revenues, and its emphasis inevitably becomes even more significant during periods of stress.

The reality is that management emphasis in organizations is placed on what is being *measured* well. Because the predominance of well-constructed measurements in some companies has focused on visible competition, that is where the day-by-day essence of management is likely to have been centered in those companies.

However, this is an era of changing market expectations, fickle customer tastes, explosive product and service commoditization, rapid corporate consolidation to increase competitive strength, and exponentially better quality, cost, and delivery improvements throughout the world. Therefore, this management of *visible* value-creation competition must be much more fully coupled in these companies with the second (and at least equally powerful) competitive way to create value: *invisible* value-creation competition. Otherwise, the first way, when done alone, can contribute to the business's bones winding up bleached on the beach, as some companies sadly demonstrated in recent years.

COMPETING BY "INVISIBLE" VALUE CREATION

This second value-creating competitive component is leadership in terms of what might be thought of as "invisible" competition, which is fundamental

- For the business success of pacesetter companies
- For its recognition in the results of astute investors when they are determining which companies they want to place their holdings in
- For the actions of well-informed customers who concentrate on buying product and service value

- For the job choices of today's "entrepreneurial employees" who want to work in an environment of prospective company growth

It is how an organization thinks, learns, decides, and, most important, acts and executes and implements. It is done in terms of maintaining the competitive strength that derives from the way an organization performs (far better than its competition) in recruiting, staffing, and motivating as well as in developing, making, selling, financing, and maintaining the company's products and services that are wanted by and affordable for its customers—and doing so with far fewer business failure costs.

"MATERIALIZING THE INTANGIBLES": KEY MANAGEMENT CAPITAL RESOURCES AND BEST PRACTICES

A fundamental factor in this leadership is to "materialize"—that is, to systematically (instead of casually) establish the company and organization "best practices"—so that

- What works well anywhere in the organization becomes quickly available everywhere in the organization
- Size is used as a strength rather than allowed to become a weakness as the company continues to grow
- Organizational "wisdom" becomes consolidated in key guidelines for aligned actions throughout the company

This *best practices component* of the company's management capital includes the knowledge, skills, learning steps, and attitudes that are the creators and implementors of these practices throughout the company. They are developed and used in all key areas of the company, including marketing, sales, financial and accounting, legal development and design, distribution and packaging, production, information technology and software, human resources, customer relations, supply and transportation, general management, and similar areas. This is fundamentally different from the emphasis in an earlier era in some companies, which focused primarily on the areas directly related to *visible competition* rather than on integrating their invisible and visible competitive strengths. These invisible strengths include, as just two of the many examples, the following:

- The product and service relationships that uniquely connect the organization with customers, especially in such areas as product and service brands (which not only provide customer recognition but also represent the company's "promise to the customer")

- The technical database and other "intangible" capital areas that are also important "invisible-to-competitors" leadership drivers

The implementation of these best practices is generated and leveraged throughout the organization in the many immediate and easy-to-use availability formats that support the work of every person in the organization. These formats range from Intranet to Internet, audiovisual, process documentation, and the many other delivery processes that meet the organizational requirements. They are themselves experiencing increasingly rapid improvement as information technology developments progress.

Pacesetter companies develop, manage, maintain, and invest in the management systems that, among their other major functions, provide the process foundation for the creation of these best practices. Without this foundation and ongoing discipline, the implementation and use of these best practices would be on an incremental, case-by-case basis, which would never meet the management criteria for best practice competitive strength.

Pacesetting companies increasingly plan for thoroughly analyzing, planning, constructing, and continuously improving the management excellence emphasis that develops and measures the processes and systems that accomplish this. What sets these companies apart is that they increasingly approach these *processes and systems* as systematically as they invest in and manage *physical capital resources.* These companies recognize that, compared to their *visible* products and services, it is difficult (if not impossible) for competitors to duplicate this *invisible* strength except over a long period of time. Moreover, some pacesetter companies increasingly consider the systems and processes for accomplishing this to be fully as much "fixed" and "semifixed" costs as are their physical capital assets, even though current accounting procedure has not yet completely developed standards for this.

AN EXAMPLE: "NATURAL" PRODUCT DEVELOPMENT CYCLES

For example, an electronic and computer products company developed an organizational wisdom "best practice" for the market-driven and customer-led "natural" product development cycle that drives all its products. This "natural" cycle serves very effectively as one of the timing-for-product-development guidelines in that company; this is important because one of the company's dominant business strategies is being first in the market. Figure 24 depicts this cycle.

The intellectual, technical, legal, customer relationship, and other best practices in this company have demonstrated that the company's customers, markets, and competitive forces take all its products through four basic market stages that are driven by basic customer and market forces. The next sections describe each stage.

Stage 1 is defined by the innovation *of the new product functions*. Buyers are initially attracted by the product's novelty. The consumer is not necessarily deterred by possible rough distribution, performance, and availability issues as long as those problems are fixed quickly. With some products the buyer may in fact take as a *positive* feature the fact that he or she is somewhat involved in assuring product operation. Strong pricing can be maintained by the company during this period and can be acceptable to the market. Profitability can be very attractive.

Stage 2 develops in terms of conspicuous consumption *of the product*. This occurs as the market expects the product to be traded up as features are added and handsome packaging becomes available. Attractability and appearance now become major factors in consumers' expectations. Although competition also becomes more powerful, pricing can remain excellent for the company and still be acceptable to buyers.

In Stage 3, **functional use,** *the product moves into widespread market absorption and into the customer's lifestyle.* The product is taken for granted in functional terms; as other products may begin to incorporate these functions, pricing becomes more and more competitive. The company can still be attractively profitable as long as it has moved toward operating cost leadership.

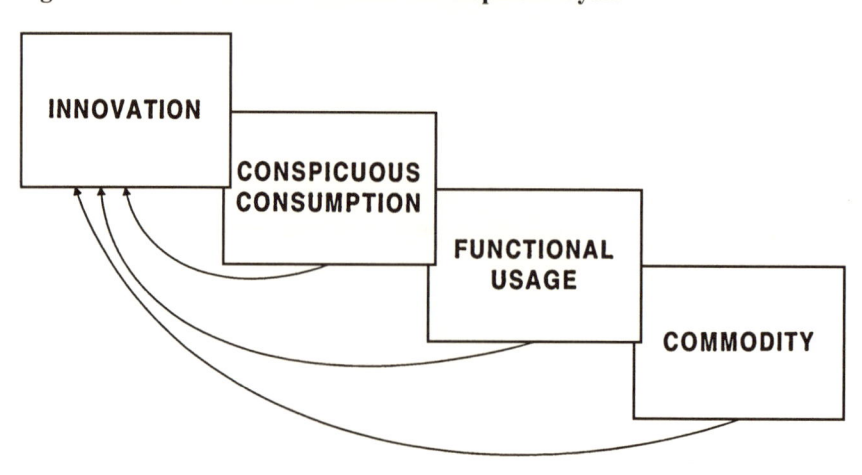

Figure 24 The "Natural" Product Development Cycle

INNOVATION → CONSPICUOUS CONSUMPTION → FUNCTIONAL USAGE → COMMODITY

TOTAL PRODUCT MATURITY CYCLE

In Stage 4, **commodity use,** *reliability and product economy are essential determinants.* This requires lead-time determination concerning possible outsourcing, dramatically different distribution or engineering, or other tactics if they are determined to fit the company's product strategy as the product becomes commoditized. Price maintenance becomes an enormous challenge.

MANAGING THE ENTIRE PRODUCT DEVELOPMENT CYCLE

At all stages a company must progressively review its decisions concerning entirely new product development, the desirability of remaining in the market to retain customer relationships, and whether to discontinue the product. For example, as "stage 2" proceeded in this company, this organizational wisdom component of management capital became increasingly valuable and influential as a tool for guiding awareness, learning, and decisions at all levels of the organization.

At all stages constant attention to decisions involving entirely new product development provides sensitivity and very important decision balance and lead-time assistance in the very careful fact-based evaluation of what actually is happening in the market. Its absence in earlier eras contributed to very strong internal pressure from functional areas of the company not to "mess with success," leading to the company staying too long with this very profitable stage 2 pattern for some of its products. This allowed more aggressive competitors to lead the way into the next stage, toward which the market was already moving, with substantial loss in market share and sales momentum for the company.

LEADERSHIP TO "BLINDSIDE" COMPETITORS

Unlike a company's products, which the competition can comparison shop, engineer, and readily track, it is far more difficult for competitors to determine how the company is *managing* to work more effectively than they are—perhaps until the impact becomes apparent in the marketplace and perhaps not in detail even then. A principal factor in this materialization of management capital is that leadership of this sort positions a company to blindside those competitors with much better results. This is true whether the competitors are in the same city or are producing on another continent. And when the company's know-how does emerge, the company already is involved in the next form of blindsiding through a relentless management emphasis of the basic operating principle that a better way to compete means positioning the company for a further better way to compete.

This emphasizes direct management focus on business sales growth and business effectiveness growth, integrated managerially from the top down, throughout the company (as discussed in Chapter 7). It is fundamentally different from the approach in which running the business to grow and improving the business's effectiveness are managed without effective alignment, coordinated priorities, organizational visibility, long-term managerial attention spans, or systematic discipline.

Effective business improvement results from using the company's management capital, to the fullest practical extent, as integral "in-line" parts of operating responsibilities themselves rather than by creating or expanding separate "off-line" components. This makes the company's management resources a companywide sum, not a case-by-case difference. The fundamental company "quality-of-management" expectation always emphasizes full alignment among all company functions—marketing, sales, distribution, production, engineering, finance, human resources, and business development actions—as a competitive advantage in itself.

This is an enormous competitive advantage in these times, when the same technology or the same product or service application can spread within a few weeks throughout companies around the world and when the same customer is the target of the marketing and sales initiatives of all those companies. The competitive impact ranges from time cycle leadership in new product and service innovation and development to down-deep organizationwide cost reduction.

AN EXAMPLE: INTEGRATING PRODUCT DEVELOPMENT PROCESSES

For example, an industrial products company has integrated its business innovation and development foundation throughout all of its product developments taking place in a global network. This integrated approach makes best practices intelligence widely available. At the same time it provides more time and resource availability to create the particular product and service developments that fit the wide range of the company's local as well as global markets. These development best practices therefore provide the company with the following benefits:

- User value marketing and sales requirements became a full and equal partner with innovation from the inception of product development.
- Simultaneous development and process matches can be made very early instead of *after* operational planning has already independently frozen the alternatives.

- Full-service suppliers become genuinely integrated partners at the beginning of development rather than an arm's-length adversarial and surveillance problem later on.
- Integration with the distribution operation can be achieved direct to the customer as part of the basic plan.

These practices originally were globally widely diverse (which is still the case with all the company's competitors), but the company now uniquely benefits from common test practices.

Total business development time cycles have been reduced as much as 80 percent in some cases because of the following clear, disciplined practices:

- Seamless up-front delivery connection with the customer
- Reduction of continuous and sometimes very late engineering and production changes
- Direct integration with short order-to-distribution cycles

Finally, global supplier content has increased more than one-third, at a much lower cost and a shorter delivery cycle. At the same time the greater speed of product and service introduction has increased international sales growth significantly.

AN EXAMPLE: HUMAN RESOURCE EFFECTIVENESS

In a further example of blindsiding, a corporation with a large number of employees in many locations established an organizationwide initiative to create best practices to improve the effectiveness of its vitally important middle level of management. The company achieved this goal by doing the following:

- Clearly defining work processes and goals
- Implementing a self-directed teamwork structure
- Clearly defining the systems and information to support the individual work units
- Instilling individual responsibility for improving processes and work team development
- Rapidly deploying improved business practices for use in other areas of the business

Comparable emphasis was placed on front-line employee results through the following procedures:

- Assuring optimum employee utilization and effectiveness through training, empowerment, involvement, and recognition
- Clearly aligning employee performance goals with business goals
- Freeing management from non-value-added tasks to rapidly compound improvement throughout the organization

The company focused on evolving toward degrees of achievement of team-based operation through empowerment growth, as is shown in Figure 25.

Typical improvements throughout various areas included the following:

- Reduced personnel turnover by 15 percent and absenteeism by 10.
- Improved safety performance by 50 percent.
- Reduced direct labor hours by 15 percent.
- Faster decision making and accelerated action, which improved the overall work flow.
- Greater acceptance of and desire for individual responsibility and accountability.
- Improved communication, less bureaucracy, and a more nimble organization.
- Greater involvement by employees in problem resolution and process improvement.

INFORMATION *MANAGEMENT:* NOT JUST INFORMATION TECHNOLOGY

One of the key ways in which pacesetter companies can produce these blindsiding results is to build the competitive strength and effectiveness of their information management channels. This is a fundamental component of management capital attitude and emphasis.

This emphasis on such systematic management of information *integration* is fundamentally different from a fascination with information *technology* in and of itself. That fascination was prevalent in some companies in the past, and it remains a competitive limitation in a few. Unfortunately, those companies have periodically experienced the following data management problems:

- Lack of data availability and timeliness
- Lack of data integrity

Figure 25 Team-Based Operation Growth

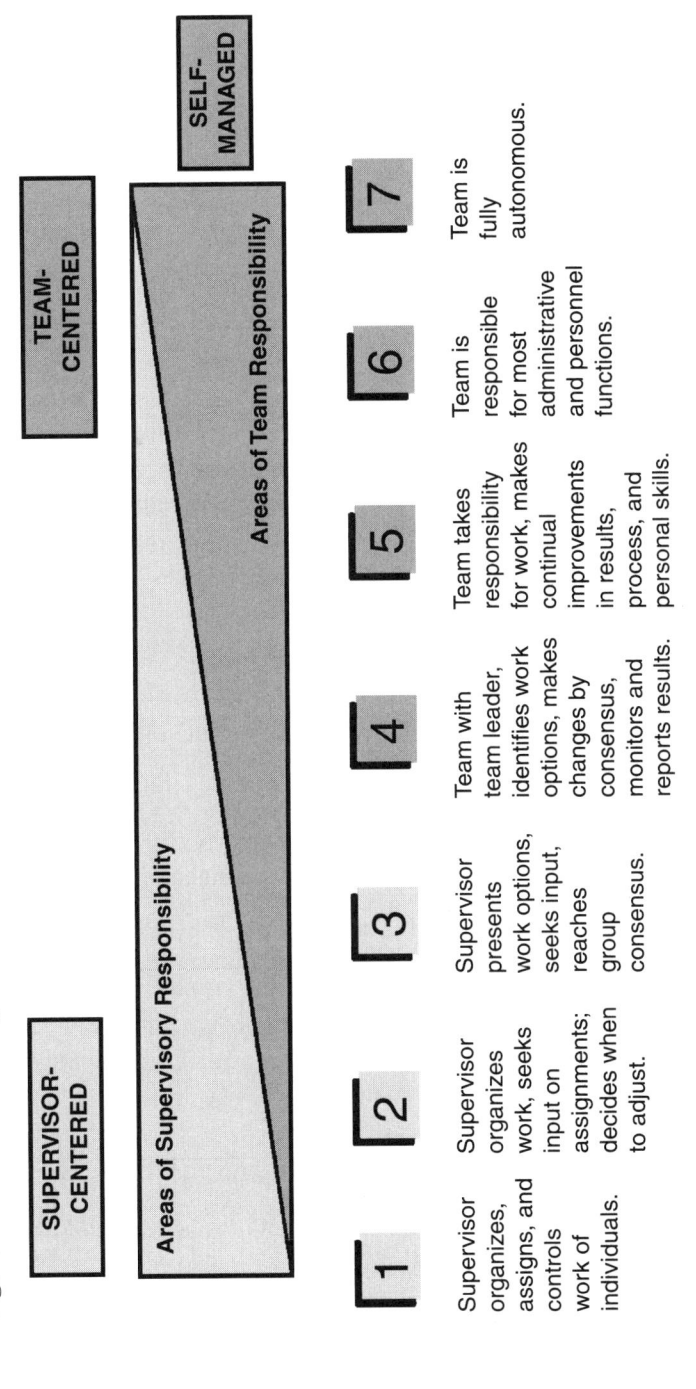

SUPERVISOR-CENTERED

TEAM-CENTERED

SELF-MANAGED

Areas of Supervisory Responsibility

Areas of Team Responsibility

1. Supervisor organizes, assigns, and controls work of individuals.

2. Supervisor organizes work, seeks input on assignments; decides when to adjust.

3. Supervisor presents work options, seeks input, reaches group consensus.

4. Team with team leader, identifies work options, makes changes by consensus, monitors and reports results.

5. Team takes responsibility for work, makes continual improvements in results, process, and personal skills.

6. Team is responsible for most administrative and personnel functions.

7. Team is fully autonomous.

- Variable accessibility of data
- Limited data consolidation ability
- Multiple databases and multiple platforms
- Inconsistent data definitions resulting in inconsistent data

Moreover, they have also experienced the following information management problems:

- Information flows and system requirements are not responsive to the business usage needs of people throughout the organization because of a lack of capacity, capability, and compatibility.
- Information management has not been fully and effectively integrated with product and operations planning.
- There has been no commonly understood vision or strategy for information management throughout the organization.
- Information management has not been effectively linked to business and operating management in time-sensitive terms.
- Business analysis has not been aligned with business units or business processes in systematic management information terms.
- Information management has been fragmented by disconnects between attention to managing *information* and attention to managing information *systems*.
- Information management has had no clear "home" in the organization.
- Information management solutions have been piecemeal and often have not been preceded by systematic fundamental business process development.
- Information technology has functioned as a technical silo with incomplete and inefficient integration with business operations.
- Information business failure and opportunity costs have not been determined or visible, understood, or directly managed as a basis for improvement and investment.

INFORMATION MANAGEMENT FOR COMPETITIVE BLINDSIDING

By comparison, the management capital emphasis of pacesetter companies systematically addresses information as an *integral* business leadership component of *management,* not as information technology as such.

This integrated information management provides an enormous competitive leadership advantage to pacesetter companies by effectively networking and diffusing high-integrity data support throughout the company infrastructure and e-frastructure. This approach is essential to provide the alignment, organizational visibility, and management attention span that are required for achieving and maintaining the superior performance results that blindside other companies in the same marketplace.

These results are achieved by efficiently integrating, maintaining, and continually upgrading the information process support of all business operations: marketing, development, production, distribution, supply, and others. The competitive leadership emphasizes increased leverage for better business results because of the following process improvements:

- Timely and consistent information for effective decision making
- Better data integrity
- Improved information flows
- Reduced information failure costs
- Selective consolidation of key business information
- Functional database management
- More positive management of the following:
    - Assets
    - Supply chain components
    - Global operations metrics
    - Planning and control results
    - Innovation data
    - Records consistency and integrity
    - Human resources data
    - Performance of quality, cycle time, and cost
    - Regulatory and environmental compliance
    - Customer needs and relationships
    - Competitive initiatives
- Of increasingly great importance, an especially rapidly growing dimension of Internet and Web business operations

AN EXAMPLE: MANAGING INFORMATION MANAGEMENT EFFECTIVENESS

For example, a key factor in the corporate strategic plan of an international producer and distributor of components was to greatly increase its competitive strength and business effectiveness; the company also wanted to significantly reduce its information costs in its functional and administrative areas. In the past the company had primarily emphasized improvements in technical upgrades on an area-by-area basis. It had paid less attention to how it managed its integrated business information effectiveness, which had begun to represent a major opportunity for improving business growth and potentially significant cost reduction.

The company therefore began to focus on clearly defined and controlled activities in the following areas:

1. Explicit management of assured quality and timeliness of information for management decisions
2. Ease of cross-functional sharing of vital information and commonality of format
3. Reduced data refresh cycle times, together with increased data availability
4. Integration and coordination of information management functions and information systems users
5. Better responsiveness and flexibility for information equipment and information management growth

The company made major improvements in the integrity, availability, and use of its data, which assisted in its business and revenue growth. In addition, over time, the company achieved significant improvement results from this strategic initiative, including the following:

- It saved $250 million in purchasing costs because of the unification of database applications and other initiatives.
- It reduced its project development costs by more than 10 percent.
- It realized significant savings from improved control of equipment use and equipment maintenance expense.
- It eliminated redundant or overlapping information management expense in business units.
- It was able to perform clearer and faster marketing and pricing analysis, which expedited customer sales results.

DEVELOPING AND MAINTAINING VISIBLE AND INVISIBLE VALUE-CREATING COMPETITIVE STRENGTH: FUNDAMENTALLY CHANGING THE LINE AND STAFF MODEL OF MANAGEMENT

What sets pacesetter companies apart is their emphasis on connecting and integrating the management of their *visible* and *invisible* value-creating competitive strength. Pacesetters recognize, develop, maintain, align, integrate, and relentlessly drive the performance excellence of this strength, and they have the leadership skill to do so. This chapter has illustrated how pacesetter companies do this effectively. They have leadership with the personal know-how and commitment for developing these results and for playing a key role in their implementation.

This approach fundamentally changes the line and staff model of traditional management, which many businesses still use today, which holds that *running* the business and *improving* the business are separate channels. Instead, this approach holds that "line" and "staff" in today's business operations (if in fact the terms are used at all) are integrated bases for achieving business results instead of having one deal with *operating* the business and the other deal with *advising* on how to operate the business. Staff is recognized as a further way to generate business results. Indeed, this model recognizes that as companies flattened organizationally in the last decade, the result was often the disappearance of the traditional corporate staff. Yet the improvement processes that underpin the integration of business sales growth and business effectiveness have become progressively more important and more effective in the twenty-first-century business climate, especially in the e-business environment.

CHAPTER 9

TEN LEADERSHIP CHARACTERISTICS FOR CAPITALIZING MANAGEMENT POWER THROUGHOUT THE BUSINESS VALUE CHAIN

THE EARLY YEARS OF THE TWENTY-FIRST CENTURY have seen one of the most deep-seated and rapid transformations of the economic and social global environment for business in many years. A great deal of the management and leadership strength that was defined by the strong growth of the recent past remains important; however, today's pacesetting business leadership is characterized by *not* depending unduly for strong business results on very good markets or on powerful technological silver bullets, although they help greatly.

During the 1990s and into the early twenty-first century a rising sea of international expansion was created by a remarkably effective combination of abundant financial resource availability, regulatory easing, strong technological growth, and acquisitions, mergers, and alliances that supported those factors. It was an era of high customer confidence and expectations, with a willingness to spend money to satisfy those expectations. Many markets were clearly sellers' markets both because of strong consumer and corporate buyer income levels and because of products and services dominated by technology that had strong demand. Those products commanded high volumes and strong pricing at the innovation and conspicuous consumption product and service levels depicted in the Figure 24 (see Chapter 8).

Business focus and management practice responded to and were defined in these growth and expansionist terms. In some companies there was a natural tendency to confuse those enormously powerful *markets* and the results they provided with enormously powerful *management*. All this, taken together, helped to raise most—if not all—business boats.

FOUR DIMENSIONS OF COMPETITIVE LEADERSHIP

By comparison, today's economy has created a very different economic, social, and global environment that is challenging business leadership. The requirement is for leading and managing successfully, systematically, and opportunistically in these demanding business conditions. The objectives are results that sustain and accelerate profitability and growth in terms that confirm a company's character and bring together its visible and invisible strengths for competitive leadership in today's brutally demanding markets.

For pacesetter companies this means establishing the overarching themes for capitalizing their management power in terms that fit their particular requirements, personality, and customer and business demands.

The importance of doing this has been summed up by a leading CEO who put that experience this way: "If it's just somebody pushing a gimmick or a program without an overarching theme, you can't get through the wall."

There is a common denominator among pacesetters in regard to focusing their management excellence process for bringing together the several initiatives discussed in earlier chapters. This common denominator has four dimensions for sustaining and accelerating their companies' profitability and growth, which are discussed in the following sections.

1. A NEW AND MORE POWERFUL EMPHASIS ON CUSTOMER VALUE LEADERSHIP FOR MARKETING AND SALES STRENGTH, INCLUDING PRODUCT AND SERVICE DEVELOPMENT THAT CREATES A LOCK ON THE FUTURE

Although customers are always number one in a company's attention, they now demand a relentless new focus in today's buyers' markets. The emphasis is on fully meeting the demands and expectations of these highly informed, extremely demanding purchasers with products and services that provide them with complete customer value satisfaction. This is true whether the purchaser is a consumer, a business customer, a human services customer, or a governmental customer.

That means satisfaction with the functions, characteristics, and appearance of a company's products and services as well as with how they are presented, sold, serviced, and supported. This is—taken together—what is meant by product and service quality today. Quality in these terms is what today's customer says it is—no more, no less—and it must be managed and measured in these terms. Moreover, it is a constantly changing target that must be tracked continually in today's brutally competitive marketplace.

Understanding and responding to this are the key to the competitive marketing and sales strength of pacesetter companies. However, for some other companies that have become distanced from their customer markets—their sales have been good, but they have lost touch with the value terms in which their customers are thinking—it can create a major hit on sales and an urgent demand for major improvement.

2. OPERATING COST LEADERSHIP FOR THE COMPANY'S ECONOMIC STRENGTH

The key here is for a company to rigorously make productive cost reduction an integral part of day-by-day leadership and management. This means a consistent and systematic emphasis on reductions in total cost by eliminating business failure costs, disconnects, and the backward creep in performance that drive unproductive results. This is a very different approach from off-and-on displays of cost cutting through "slash-and-burn cost reduction" that can eliminate strong and highly productive activities along with unproductive ones.

3. MANAGEMENT INNOVATION AND TOTAL RESOURCE USE FOR COMPETITIVE BUSINESS IMPROVEMENT

The emphasis here is on meeting the considerable challenge of structuring and systematizing management innovation. Companies must recognize that major business improvement means a better way to lead and manage the business that at the same time positions the company for a *further* better way to run the business. In pacesetter companies the results are now measured in clear financial terms to recognize these major management innovation improvements. Major business improvement expands and modernizes the traditional cost-accounting measurement of physical hard-asset-driven results, which once was thought of as the only corporately acceptable measurement of improvement, while everything else was reported as being "for memorandum purposes only." That approach often drew management and resource attention *away* from many other truly significant areas for competitive leadership.

This management innovation becomes a fundamental way of life and a major competitive advantage for a company. It provides an enormous business strength for leadership in *systematically*—rather than *incrementally*—dealing with today's improvement imperative, as was discussed in Chapter 5. This management innovation and improvement imperative entails a particular focus on the following areas:

- Global expansion
- Time cycle compression
- Customer satisfaction
- Managing information technology
- Product and service innovation
- Material flow, logistics, and inventory management
- Quality
- Asset monetization
- Environmental demands
- Risk management

This management innovation and improvement imperative also focuses on the Internet as a digitized management innovation opportunity, particularly in terms of manufacturing and production; marketing and sales; supply; malls and exchanges; and customer, dealer, and user-participant product development networks (as discussed in detail in Chapter 5).

It is a principal competitive leadership opportunity for success in twenty-first-century companies. The parallel situation occurs when companies systematize and make *technology*—and the corresponding product and service development—into a way of life and an organizationwide mindset instead of managing product and service development as the output of a "research and development laboratory," which often results in a "time-to-time flash and revelation" approach. That, of course, has been one of the leadership success areas that differentiated several of the twentieth century's corporate leaders from their competitors.

4. EMPOWERING A COMPANY CULTURE OF SUPERIOR PERFORMANCE

This dimension of competitive leadership focuses on the effectiveness with which the passion, populism, and disciplined responsibility of management leadership are channeled and articulated to empower organizationwide energy. It is this energy through which the company's resources are integrated, networked, and deployed to sustain and accelerate profitability and growth throughout the company's key management capital channels.

As was discussed in Chapter 3, these management channels particularly involve the following areas:

- New product and service development and introduction
- Marketing effectiveness
- Business expansion and globalization
- Total quality
- Management measurement
- Partnership and alliance development
- Operations effectiveness
- Supply management
- Human resource effectiveness
- Integrated business information
- Financial operations effectiveness
- Asset management

CAPITALIZING MANAGEMENT STRENGTH FOR IMPLEMENTING THESE FOUR DIMENSIONS OF COMPETITIVE LEADERSHIP

What sets pacesetters apart is their unwavering emphasis on—and their skill in—capitalizing their management strength to develop and implement these four dimensions of today's competitive leadership:

- Customer value leadership
- Operating cost leadership
- Management innovation and total resource utilization
- Company culture of superior performance

This strength then enables these companies to sustain and accelerate profitability and growth in the company's quality of management excellence process.

In determining this result in these companies, 10 key characteristics of this leadership skill stand out. The remainder of this chapter discusses nine of these skills; Chapter 10 discusses the tenth.

LEADERSHIP CHARACTERISTIC 1: Personal Senior Leadership of the Company Quality-of-Management Excellence Process

The first characteristic is knowledgeable, hands-on leadership and development by senior management. These leaders take major, ongoing, and personal roles to create and maintain the company's quality-of-management excellence process. This leadership should *not* involve just periodic management review with specialized staffs that create this process. Moreover, leadership means *ongoing* involvement throughout the tensions that are inevitable in the company during the implementation and continuous evolution and development of this process.

This is senior management leadership with a clear vision for improvement; it also recognizes that an organization's culture is the collective result of the organization's actions—no more, no less. These leaders understand that this culture can be effected only by a bias for *hands-on* execution and implementation of these actions. This is leadership with a deep confidence in the capabilities of employees throughout the organization to bring about these changes, which creates an organizationwide atmosphere of superior performance and recognizes that the pursuit of excellence is the most powerful emotional motivator in any organization. It is leadership with a sureness and lightness of touch, leadership that understands that a good management process, like a good stomach, works best when one scarcely knows that it is there.

Moreover, what particularly causes pacesetter companies to stand apart from their competitors is the major *personal time* and *commitment* to the quality-of-management excellence process among senior leaders, especially in the face of the many demands on their time. This is a key to their enormous advantage in effectiveness compared with some of their competitors that depend for process creation and maintenance on specialized staffs of unquestionably high competence. These staffs would certainly welcome and benefit from this strong direct senior management involvement; however, it is sometimes absent because of the other demands placed on management time.

LEADERSHIP CHARACTERISTIC 2: A Clear Focus on the Business Model That Capitalizes the Company's Management Strength

The second key characteristic of pacesetter leadership is emphasis on and attitudes for clearly establishing twenty-first-century business models. As was discussed in earlier chapters, these models should effectively and productively network and diffuse the company's full capabilities to build a competitively strong infrastructure and e-frastructure to sustain and accelerate the business's growth.

This leadership characteristic capitalizes the company's management strength for powerful business results in terms of fully effective use of its total resources: hard physical assets and financial resources as well as soft assets (such as human resources, technology, customer and supplier relations, brand strength, and quality results, among others). It effectively integrates the company's visible and invisible competitive strengths and provides for structuring of the framework for this integration and for its leadership and management.

LEADERSHIP CHARACTERISTIC 3: Structuring the Framework for Fully Productive Use of the Company's Total Resources

The third characteristic is structuring the *process* for implementing this. This process should fit the company's business demands, and it should focus, assist, and energize everyone throughout the organization in using the company's total resources in the most complete and productive way. This is leadership that understands how to develop and clarify this focusing of the business model in the framework of

- Strategic planning
- Business planning
- Annual operating plans

- Alignment of business objectives
- Performance management and alignment
- Managing company strengths

Each of these functions is discussed in detail in the following sections.

Strategic Planning

Strategic planning is an ongoing interactive process that generates the key objectives for the company. These objectives should address the overarching demands of customer value leadership, operating cost leadership, management innovation, total resource use, and the company's culture of superior performance. Strategic planning translates those demands into a set of integrated, major strategies that recognize and opportunistically develop the business potential provided by the company's range of identified improvement imperatives. Those improvement imperatives may pertain to global expansion, time cycle compression, customer satisfaction, and other areas discussed in earlier chapters.

The strategic planning process is keyed to hard data, including financial forecasts, market analyses, competitive analyses, and internal and external assessments of the company's businesses and their strategic business units. Strategic planning then focuses on assessing the resources required to take the company to where it wants to be. The process is fundamental to differentiating the company by developing, recognizing, measuring, and deploying its full range of hard and soft assets as a major competitive advantage in itself. It also frames the focus for identifying and effectively responding and "counter punching" to what might develop as unintended consequences of the strategic planning.

Business Planning

This process develops the plans that implement the major strategies of the company and its businesses throughout the company's management-capital channels, which, as we stated in earlier chapters, include new product and service development and introduction, marketing effectiveness, partnership and alliance development, and others. The process links the *strategic planning* process with the *annual operating plan,* which is discussed in the next section. Business planning spans a time frame of months to years, depending on the strategy; it is also event-driven rather than only calendar-driven. Business planning is critical to getting people throughout the organization to develop initiatives and to explicitly network, diffuse, and integrate the company's hard and soft resources for their implementation.

Annual Operating Plan

This is the group of actions, accountabilities, and drivers required to implement the business plans. The annual operating plan takes into account the objectives, priorities, assumptions, accountabilities, and performance measurements developed in business planning.

Business Objectives Alignment

This is the process that translates the objectives, key drivers, targets, and constraints identified during the business and operating planning processes into an integrated set of actions. These actions should eliminate failure costs while simultaneously implementing operating results and providing genuine employee involvement and integration. These objectives, key drivers, targets, and resource constraints should be communicated on a "360-degree basis" that provides broad participation throughout the organization. The business objectives alignment process is used to create action plans and individual performance agreements that describe everyone's role in achieving the company's overall objectives. Roles should be described for each individual as well as for each division, facility, and department.

Performance Management and Alignment

These are the processes that link day-to-day operations with strategy. Performance management and alignment provides systematic reviews of performance indicators; it also should involve the issuing of reports to compare performance *results* with *planned* performance, indicating whether corrective action is required and focusing on realignment requirements that will eliminate disconnects.

Direct Focus on Managing and Matrixing Company Strengths—Both Invisible and Visible

These are the processes that identify, utilize, recognize, develop, and identify their management for integrating the suitable company resources and getting blindsiding competitive benefit from them. One of these processes—Matrix II—is for the *invisible* strengths of the company (as discussed in Chapter 8), such as the power of the unique competitive capabilities of the company's strategic structure itself and of its strong legal and patenting positioning. The other process—Matrix I—is for bringing together the *visible* strengths as reflected in products and services and facilities.

Figure 26 illustrates an example of the structuring of the powerful business framework in a global corporation with a wide variety of products and services in many markets. Figure 27 relates this to an example of the significant favorable results of this structure, which are regularly rolled up into the profitability of the company: 7 percent increased annual revenue after one year of installation and 17 percent after two years. In terms of operating cost savings, this amounts to 5 percent in one year and 15 percent in two years.

LEADERSHIP CHARACTERISTIC 4: Clear, Firm Goals and Organizationwide Involvement in Developing and Implementing Those Goals

The fourth leadership characteristic is integral to the first three and is a necessary complement to their success. It is the relentless focus on establishing clear and firm goals, which are necessary to sustain and accelerate a company's profitability and growth. These goals are developed and shaped by the company's character, culture, and quality-of-management leadership attitude. As was discussed in detail in Chapter 3, this attitude encompasses leadership *passion, populism*, and *disciplined responsibility*, which affect the company's goals in the following ways:

Leadership passion emphasizes establishing stretch goals—but still realistic goals—that position the company for continuing competitive leadership.

Leadership populism focuses on developing those goals, as much as possible, by means of inputs from the employees throughout the organization who are closest to the work and the customers. This input is useful because the employees often know best where the improvements can be made and how to make those improvements. They are the keys to the successful implementation of the company's goals however those goals may have been initiated.

Finally, *disciplined responsibility* requires developing goals through systematic patterns that fit the company in order to accomplish the following:

- Rigorously identify major business opportunities and issues (such as the 10 improvement imperative areas discussed earlier) in principal management capital channels that influence top-line growth and bottom-line profitability.
- Clearly establish both the physical and the financial hard-asset elements as well as the soft-asset elements (e.g., technology, human resources, market and customer relationships, and patent and brand management), which are the basis for performance in the channels.
- Determine the *strengths* (in terms of results in the management channel) and *weaknesses* (in terms of disconnects, the corresponding

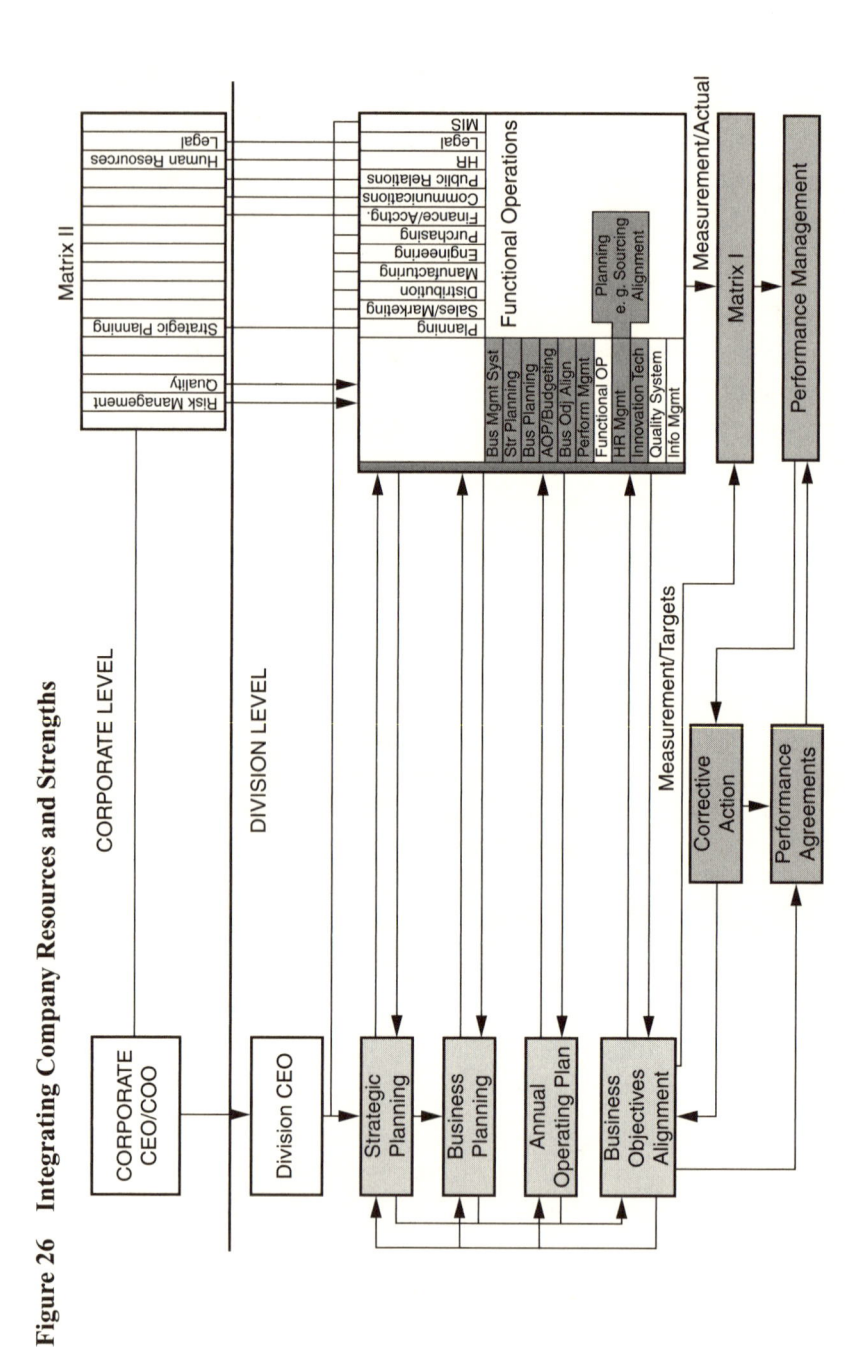

Figure 26 Integrating Company Resources and Strengths

CHAPTER 9 TEN LEADERSHIP CHARACTERISTICS   167

Figure 27 Results of Structuring

INCREASED ANNUAL REVENUE

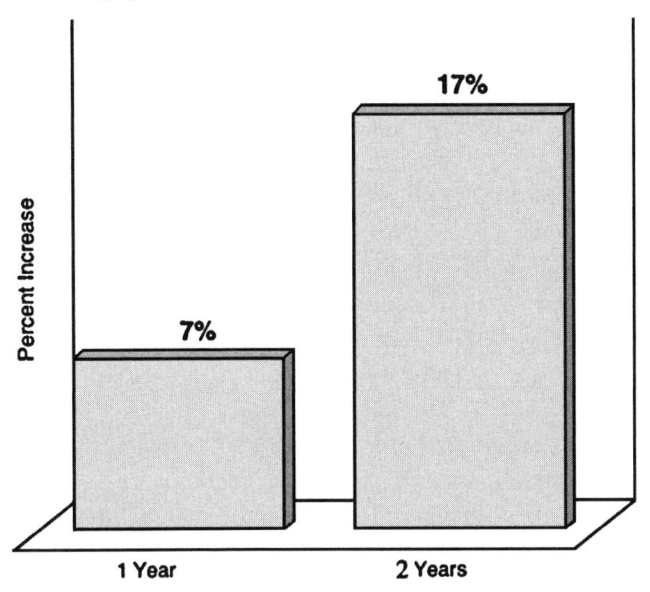

- 1 Year: 7%
- 2 Years: 17%

(Percent Increase)

OPERATING COSTS SAVINGS

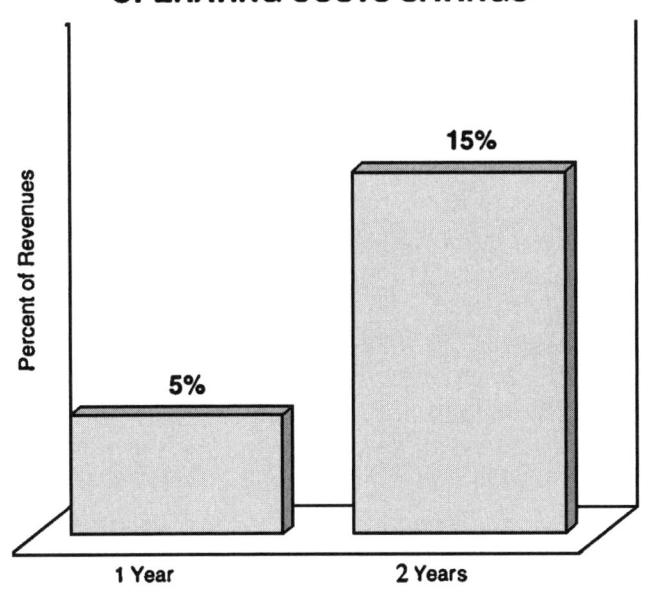

- 1 Year: 5%
- 2 Years: 15%

(Percent of Revenues)

- end-to-end systems demands, and the business costs) that are keys to implementing this growth and performance.
- Rigorously establish the patterns reconnecting disconnects and developing and improving the systems and processes that guide the full range of improvement initiatives. These systems and processes provide end-to-end, sequentially related, how-to-do-it action-based steps targeted toward specific performance results. The systems are the grouping of system process components that support the management channel results.
- Assure that this disciplined responsibility includes aggressively identifying and using global best practices, especially by means of emphasizing that what works well *anywhere* in the company is quickly available *everywhere* in the organization where it is applicable.

An Example: Improved Management of a Company's Assets

One example of this discipline in today's challenging markets is asset management. For instance, consider the experience of a company whose basic businesses are the design, manufacturing, and sales of a wide range of specialized components both for direct sale and for original equipment manufacturer (OEM) markets. Although the company was strong and profitable, it saw a significant business benefit in setting new goals for its asset utilization in light of its currently more limited markets. It recognized that its production and distribution assets had grown substantially over a period of years on a major acquisition-by-acquisition basis. This was in accordance with its policy of "complete readiness and availability to serve" in response to the major increases in its international markets.

Analysis under those new market conditions showed an increasing number of slow periods in which a very high proportion of assets were determined to be "awaiting use" for very rapid response to the just-in-time demands of customers and for quick design changeover alterations in the more specialized market segments. A significant proportion of assets was designated as "unavailable" during those periods because of changeover and possible retention of old equipment "just in case of possible use."

However, changed market conditions now made it possible, through improved scheduling, to make much of this response to customers less necessary; this also made it uneconomical to retain older equipment. Furthermore, the proportion of equipment in preventive maintenance could be better scheduled and transferred from that "awaiting use" or "unavailable" through changes in traditional maintenance scheduling practices that had not taken possible flexibility into account.

This company effectively implemented improvements that corresponded with the goals it had set: Figure 28 shows the significant 15 percent improvement in asset utilization achieved in this case.

LEADERSHIP CHARACTERISTIC 5: Emphasis on Execution, Implementation, Innovation, Reducing Distance, and Eliminating Disconnects and Failure Costs

The fifth characteristic is leadership that emphasizes the importance of implementation and constant innovation. This structuring of the framework for the full use of resources and the establishment of the goals for their implementation, while a necessary condition for sustaining and accelerating the results of the business, is genuinely successful only through such highly effective implementation and execution. This is reflected in the 12- to 24-month actions whose results are shown in Figure 27. It is leadership that recognizes that structure and goals are not effective without the corresponding *tactics* and that neither will generate strong and positive business results without effective *implementation.* Packaged together, tactics and implementation are the full business egg; separately, they are just the white and the yolk.

This is leadership that understands the organizationwide imperative for accomplishing this in ways that eliminate the disconnects and the corre-

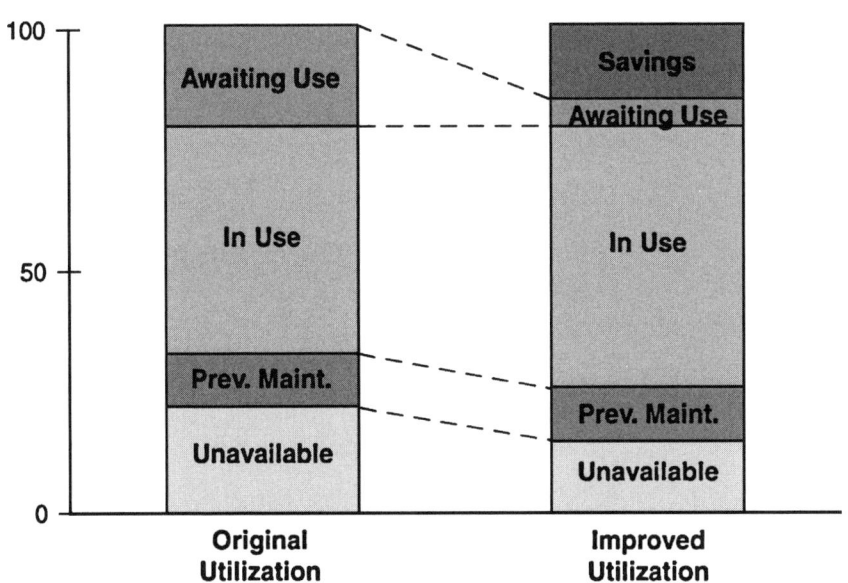

Figure 28   Asset Utilization Improvement

sponding failure costs that have progressively blunted integrated resource strengths in some companies. This is leadership that recognizes the importance of establishing the enabling strength of the company's management capital for management innovation in all key value-creating competitive areas from financial effectiveness to customer satisfaction and service.

This kind of leadership closes the distance between company management and employees throughout the organization. It is far different from the central planning and strategic planner focus through which many companies progressively *increased* that distance from employees. It is the kind of leadership that works very hard at closing the equally critical distance between employees and the company's customers.

Its management style is a hands-on focus coupled with the purging of worn-out management doctrines that may remain within the company. Its focus is on the global emphasis that connects the company with the here-and-now business environment (i.e., world markets, customer developments, employee attitudes, supplier trends, and investor and public expectations). It is the kind of leadership whose *actions* create structure and organization—*not* the architecturally elegant (but ineffective)organization charts and thick books of management procedures of so many companies in the past.

LEADERSHIP CHARACTERISTIC 6: Creating an Environment of Positive Attitude and Opportunistic Involvement

The sixth leadership skill entails developing an environment of positive attitudes and opportunistic involvement that makes all these results possible. It is characterized by recognition that in many business periods in the past, employees throughout organizations often regarded the status quo as their friend and a protector of employment and compensation and regarded *change* of many types as their enemy. More recently, however, employees have seen many companies lose their competitive position when the necessary leadership and improvement have not been present. Experience correspondingly shows that today's employees can learn to accept the status quo as their *enemy* and view change and opportunistic improvement as their *friend*—that is, *when* their knowledge, skills, and attitudes become deeply involved in developing and implementing this change.

When led in these terms, an organization develops great resilience in responding and making improvements even when faced with many existing projects, thinness of personnel, and the skepticism about change that can characterize companies in these times. The biggest error in the leadership of some of these companies has been to underestimate this resilience and to lack the necessary confidence in the strength of employees to become part of change when they can contribute to and understand it and can see potential personal benefits from it.

The vision of the company is fundamental in creating this positive attitude and opportunistic involvement for creating a common focus. Such visioning must be an ongoing process for creating a common focus in the face of implementation difficulties. Among the many examples was Microsoft's vision that "we will own the desktop," which built the company and helped it dominate first operating systems and then applications software. In the face of the major challenges it continues to face, Microsoft, with strong and continuing future focus, is now depending on its Internet vision—among other things—as one of the powerhouses of change to integrate and focus positive attitudes and opportunistic involvement within the company and throughout its business value chain.

Furthermore, effective and constant communication is essential to achieve this goal. Employees can generally deal with *bad* organization news if they have some chance to be informed about it, react to it, talk about it, and understand it. They can certainly readily absorb good news. What creates communications problems with improvement initiatives is dealing with *no* news—when employees do not know or think they do not know what is taking place.

Finally, business is timing, and speed is essential for effective improvement. The common management learning experience of companies and their leadership during this decade has been that the single biggest error of some companies is that they have moved too slowly in implementation—not too fast.

LEADERSHIP CHARACTERISTIC 7: Improvement Empowerment through Organization Flexibility and Training

This characteristic does not only emphasize increasing employee responsibility step by step at the workplace; instead, it uses a far more basic approach that recognizes today's new economic and social environment. This type of leadership goes well beyond the approach of earlier years, which was often termed "empowerment." That approach usually meant a *piecemeal* increase in some job responsibilities without the necessary genuine *management* and *resource* changes that provide the foundation for real improvement, and its payoff was correspondingly highly limited.

Quality-of-management leadership creates the power of an environment of trust, openness, and honest communication to encourage the development of what we have described as "individual job entrepreneurs." This leadership uses the company's management capital structure and processes to support that environment.

This means providing full opportunity for employees throughout the workforce to develop their own forms of analysis and of teamwork and benchmarking improvement. An increasing number of people in the company workforce today—together with the often decentralized character and the use of Internet communication—bring a great new potential to improve the quality of work in organizations. This improvement is realized when there is genuine support and recognition in the company of processes that encourage the fundamental knowledge, skills, and attitudes of those people to solve problems democratically, network with each other as members of a learning organization, achieve genuinely constant improvement, and be trained to organize and deliver results on this basis.

For business effectiveness, such training becomes integral in everybody's job throughout the organization. Our experience with many companies indicates that the process and management structure that emphasizes this integration is the key to making the all-important role of training fully effective, in comparison to the self-contained organization silo that training programs have become in some companies.

LEADERSHIP CHARACTERISTIC 8: Rigorous Emphasis on Short-Term as Well as Long-Term Goals

The need for clear short-term goals and their full realization has always been recognized as a fundamental dimension of corporate growth. After all, there is no long term without the short term in business. Short-term goals are of equal importance as a key component of expanding personal involvement in the management excellence process.

A fundamental reason for the importance of short-term goals is that only the visible and tangible help for employees' work that comes from some early improvements will convince employees (as well as some members of management) of the reality and value of the relentless stretch goals, the improvement initiative, and the importance and value of employees' full connection with and involvement in the improvement initiative. This demand for consistent awareness of these improvement results is a fundamental determinant of the constancy of the improvement initiative.

High-visibility improvements show early success and build momentum. As the improvement capability, competence, and commitment of the organization's employees increase, expansion of involvement in the improvement process positions the organization for the next action.

LEADERSHIP CHARACTERISTIC 9: Emphasis on Productive Partnerships and Alliances throughout the Company Value Chain

The ninth leadership characteristic that defines the management excellence process is the ability to establish continuously better and more productive relationships not only with suppliers but also with the many other organizations that are important to the success and growth of a company. Today's demanding times require such new and more effective economic partnerships and alliances.

One key area for this is the recognition of the importance of an emphasis on supplier flexibility, willingness, and ability to pitch in with quick help to the company's value network that is strongly emerging as one of the basic keys to profitability. This emphasis is changing the arm's-length, squeeze-the-supplier approach of the past to the full and open cooperation approach required by the rapidly changing, increasingly volatile business conditions of the global marketplace.

Today's demanding conditions create the need to make more manageable and more effective some fundamentally important key business strategies, such as the following:

- Full-service supply concepts
- Integration of increasing numbers of components by a single supplier
- Shorter or just-in-time deliveries between global companies
- Vendor-managed inventory throughout the supply chain

Companies are now recognizing successful examples of this emphasis on partnering. Among them is the remarkably rapid five-day recovery of a major Japanese automobile company from a fire that wiped out one of its large factories. This factory was the only one that produces most of the brake-fluid proportioning "P" valves for some automotive models, which support the production of 14,000 cars a day in 20 of the company's car plants. The company was able to recover quickly because of its suppliers' flexibility and responsiveness.

These relationships also include new forms of cooperation with organizations that are strong competitors in some other markets. Joint business processes with those organizations now permit better joint use of resources. They make possible lower costs and greater efficiency in joint development, marketing, and distribution of certain products and services while a company continues to engage in fierce end-product competition with the partner in some other business areas. This is one of the keys today to a successful and growing company rather than one that just spends a lot of money on organization building. It emphasizes the principle that one should continuously evaluate the case-by-case circumstances for owning, in one's own company, only the assets whose output, quality, cost, and delivery one can operate and control best rather than obtaining them through partnering and alliances.

The tenth characteristic of leadership of the management excellence process—*recognition that the customer, not Wall Street, delivers a business's income*—is discussed in Chapter 10.

CHAPTER 10

THE CUSTOMER—
NOT WALL STREET—
DELIVERS THE
BUSINESS'S INCOME

ARLIER CHAPTERS DESCRIBED A PRIMARY CHARACTERISTIC of pacesetting companies that sustain and accelerate their profitability and growth in good times and bad. That characteristic is their understanding of—and respect for and responsiveness to—today's very well-informed and extremely demanding customer; it also involves their know-how in regard to accomplishing this.

Chapters 1 through 9 discussed management capital as businesses' overarching theme for capitalizing the management power of their total resources, soft as well as hard. Management capital implements innovation for relentlessly increasing value for all of a company's constituencies, especially its customers, whose satisfaction with the company's products and services is the key to this customer responsiveness.

THE MARKET POWER OF COMPLETE CUSTOMER VALUE SATISFACTION

The market business power of customer satisfaction is demonstrated by data showing that in consumer products, customers who are highly satisfied with a company's quality are four times more likely to buy from that company again than they are to buy from its competitors. In business and industrial products, they are seven times more likely to buy. This is a price-assisted judgment, sometimes assisted by the Internet, which can make a company's product and service quality immediately transparent and greatly escalate the quantity and leverage of these favorable and unfavorable numbers.

Of course, strongly positive results for a business's other stakeholders—i.e., investors, employees, suppliers, and the public—are essential. The very successful CEO of one large global corporation made this point about serving the full range of his constituency during a major platform address; he then made an additional remark (near a still-open microphone), stating that although what he had said was completely true, the *customer* was the 800-pound gorilla on whose shoulders all the rest of those constituencies were being carried and who made positive results for them possible. He kept this in mind every morning when he came to work to make investment and other decisions.

A key characteristic of the management excellence process in pacesetter companies is leadership that recognizes that the customer—not Wall Street—delivers the company's income and that Wall Street also recognizes this through the evidence of the company's strong customer revenue growth with the corresponding profitability results.

Inability to achieve leadership in these balanced terms has unfortunately been a key reason for the decline of many organizations in recent years.

EMPHASIS ON CUSTOMER SATISFACTION AND QUALITY

Of course, the way each company determines how to achieve this customer leadership depends on the particular conditions of its markets, pricing, product and service maturity, global competitive forces, and a host of other differentiators that define the individual conditions of each company. However, experience shows that there are common denominators that are the foundations for establishing the necessary initiatives. They basically focus on the quantification of answers to fundamental questions such as the following:

- How can we make our consumer customers continually *more satisfied* and *more secure* (the safety question) through what they buy from us?
- How can we make our business and industrial customers *more competitive* through what they buy from us?

From the customers' point of view, the results of this come together at the point of sale in terms of the definition of and the expectation for quality through which customers judge the products and services of a company. That is taking place in the new, highly demanding global marketplaces in which twenty-first-century companies must operate and compete.

QUALITY IN TODAY'S MARKETS

A primary characteristic of quality in these markets is the fact that buyers' expectations and tastes have been changing quickly as fewer and fewer people are willing to accept being anything less than first-class in their lives, in the products they buy and the services they use, and in the working practices of which they are a part. Millions of consumers, together with tens of thousands of purchasing agents in industrial companies, also now buy in different forms of common markets and trading zones throughout the world with increasingly demanding quality requirements.

Buying patterns throughout these major U.S. and international markets show that these buyers are no longer thinking of or buying only in terms of the functions, dimensions, or characteristics of a product or the attributes of a service. Instead, they are *integrating* quality with value. They are approaching quality as a fundamental buying discipline measured by their total value perception of the product or service whose purchase they are considering as well as of the organization, delivery, and maintenance network that provides and supports it. This is what we call *perceived quality.*

This perceived quality buying discipline is expressed in the increasingly clear definitions and demands of these buyers for quality value that is increasingly moving toward three characteristics of products and services:

- They have to be essentially perfect.
- They have to be economically affordable.
- They have to be customer-determined because quality is what the *customer*—not the company—says it is.

Our surveys and research and operating systems installations are correspondingly reflecting a rapidly growing divergence between some customers and some companies in regard to customer satisfaction measurements. Some companies, in good faith and accurately based on their data, continue to state to the media as well as to customers that those data show that their quality has improved greatly—in terms of *defect reduction.* However, Internet and other marketplace customer surveys show that some buyers in the same markets state that quality has not improved at all—in terms of *increasing quality value.* This is why certain automobiles, computers, and consumer appliances with low defect rates nonetheless have generated poor sales results that have confounded the producing and merchandising companies. It is also why dealing effectively with the lack of increasing quality value is now an important part of quality activity.

SUCCESSFUL MARKET ALIGNMENT REQUIRES A FOCUS ON ENHANCING QUALITY *VALUE*

This experience makes it clear that successful market alignment of a company's customer quality leadership program now requires focusing customer satisfaction strategy on objectives and results for enhanced quality value, not primarily reacting to them on a defect reduction basis (zero or otherwise), the traditional approach to quality improvement in some organizations.

This value-enhancement objective is a fundamentally different business quality goal to drive the company's processes ranging from product and service design and development to measurement of customer satisfaction. For many companies, aligning their quality strategies to successful twenty-first-century operation now requires a basic transformation in their *management* orientation and their quality *systems* if they are going to be able to compete successfully.

The impact of this is that companies committed to quality can no longer focus their quality programs primarily on the reduction of defects or of things gone wrong for their customers. Defect reduction has become an entry-level requirement for effective quality-improvement initiatives. Today the requirement is for companies to build their quality programs throughout the customer value chain by integrating and connecting all key quality work processes; this integration uses the full strength of the company and its suppliers to increase the value of the number of things that go *right* for customers in terms of performance, service, design, and economy.

The key is a constant emphasis on quality vitality as a center point of the kind of customer leadership that drives growth. At the same time companies must *never* allow backsliding into the bureaucratic approach in which quality management sometimes meant documentation and manuals on the shelf and streams of quality audits, but without the vitality connected to the customer and to the business of the company.

The Internet has expanded this recognition of the emphasis on quality value by making the seller's quality very quickly transparent to the buyer. In Internet business much of the devil is in the details of managing the creation and the details of customer quality processes. Companies that went to market before they fully and adequately understood, strategized, and structured their Internet processes make that the number one point throughout their businesses as they continue to develop and improve their Internet operations.

This experience indicates that the Internet can magnify the buyer sales impact of a company's quality value—either up or down—to a far higher degree than is the case in the situation-by-situation buyer satisfaction or dissatisfaction pattern of traditional established brick-and-mortar businesses. The same principle in a different business framework applies to volume sales in e-business supplier-to-user exchanges and mall developments. The relative bargaining power of the buyers and sellers is likely to be a major factor in negotiating the original patterns of the exchange, but it is likely to be quality, cost, and performance that will determine the ongoing pattern and the way business is allocated.

TODAY'S MARKETS DEMAND STRATEGIC, TECHNICAL, AND OPERATIONAL ALIGNMENT OF CUSTOMER QUALITY VALUE THROUGHOUT THE ORGANIZATION

These powerful new markets require equally powerful business leadership that continuously aligns and integrates this customer value satisfaction throughout all aspects of structuring the company's business strategically as well as technically and operationally. One business characteristic that sets pacesetter companies apart today is that they lead, manage, and systematically structure quality as a fundamental strategy for continuous customer quality alignment with hands-on senior management leadership. These pacesetter companies further benefit from the strategic and technical strength provided by continuous systems engineering improvement of their companies' quality processes.

Total quality management and its effectiveness were discussed in Chapter 2 and are extended by six sigma practices *integrated* with total quality management.

This is a basically different management model from that of companies that always recognized quality as important but understood and managed quality solely in terms of a technical, operational emphasis and strong standards, with periodic upward reporting to senior management. One of the hazards of that model in today's fast-moving markets can be the many forms of customer quality disconnects and backward creep that are outcomes of situations in which the company has adhered to its internal standards but lack of timely strategic quality alignment has created quality problems. Those problems result from lack of integration with the rapidly changing customer value expectations driven by today's explosive markets.

Major challenges in accomplishing all this remain for many companies. For example, consider a report by Jeffrey E. Garten, dean of the Yale School of Management, in *Business Week*.[1] He writes that "among the 40 top business leaders interviewed for an upcoming book, the word *quality* wasn't mentioned once as a major strategic challenge."

However, today's demanding markets in fact and experience make quality an enormous competitive advantage for companies that approach it strategically. The key is to build bridges among the diverse quality improvement islands that have come to exist in many companies. Those bridges

[1] *Business Week*, December 18, 2001, p. 32.

make a company's management of quality resources a sum, not a difference. They also provide a competitive foundation for customer quality *value* and quality marketplace *alignment*, which drive complete customer *satisfaction*, which in turn creates *profitability and growth* in today's markets.

AN EXAMPLE: THE SALES AND PROFITABILITY GROWTH RESULTS OF STRATEGIC QUALITY MANAGEMENT

The CEO of a large multimarket corporation, who has led this strategic quality transition, explained the business results achieved by his company as a result of such strong customer value satisfaction. He emphasized three big improvements that it brought to his company.

First, the integrated strategic, technical, and operational alignment of quality helped create significant company sales growth because of increasing customer satisfaction, which also reduced the costs of complete quality satisfaction to 5 percent and sometimes much less as a percentage of sales revenue. This is in comparison to flatter sales results and what sometimes can amount to 20 percent and more in the costs of complete customer quality satisfaction in less well-aligned competitor businesses.

Second, the use of management leadership time has been improved greatly as a result of what the CEO described as the "reduction of 'wattless' energy created by unnecessary quality hassles in several departments of the company." He was referring to an earlier situation in which he periodically had to become engaged in helping "to drive the nails back into the quality management platforms that too regularly had been popping out in the form of areas of customer dissatisfaction, recalls, and other disconnects."

Third, the company originally found itself with quality programs increasingly dependent on individual quality improvement islands—for example, in design, production, supply, and customer service—that were not well connected with each other. Of greater concern was the fact that because of the lack of companywide integration, those quality programs were increasingly disconnected from the new quality *expectations* of customers. Because of this lack of integration, the total quality systems effectiveness of these organizations had been in the effectiveness range of 40 to 50 percent, making them increasingly vulnerable to customer dissatisfaction, high quality failure costs, and unacceptably slow product development time cycles. By comparison, by giving the company's quality system a "physical" through the analysis-planning-construction disciplines (as discussed in Chapter 6), the company now operates with the customers' satisfaction power of 90 percent systems effectiveness that now characterizes its seamless, end-to-end quality processes.

Taken together, the results over a two- to three-year period have shown significant improvements in complete customer satisfaction performance. This includes performance in such key areas as customer value satisfaction, company satisfaction capability (the key measurement of the company's capability for delivering satisfaction), satisfaction improvement performance, and the satisfaction index aggregate.

Figure 29 illustrates this customer satisfaction performance.

The consequences of these improvements have shown results in the following areas:

- Customer satisfaction leadership in each of the served markets
- Market share leadership through very high retention and loyalty and with much higher profitability than that of the nearest competitor
- Employee fulfillment through the ability to better serve customers more effectively and with a high level of job satisfaction

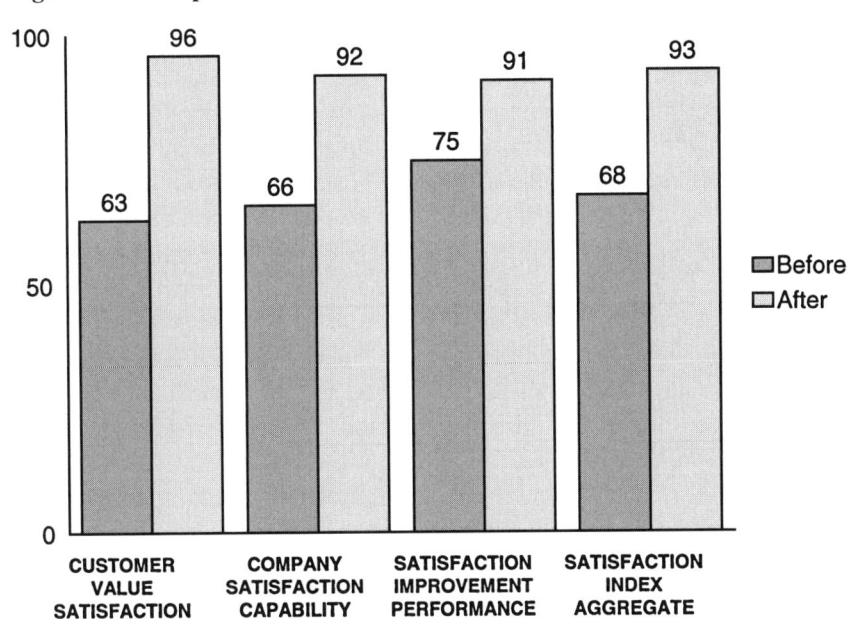

Figure 29 Complete Customer Satisfaction Results

Category	Before	After
Customer Value Satisfaction	63	96
Company Satisfaction Capability	66	92
Satisfaction Improvement Performance	75	91
Satisfaction Index Aggregate	68	93

- Significant reduction in costs to provide this customer satisfaction

It has involved continuing rigorous attention to the following areas:

- Managing the customer interface
- Motivating and recognizing the employees who work directly on the customer interface function
- Developing employee customer relations skills
- Managing customer interactions and communications
- Analyzing and managing customer complaints
- Managing customer information
- Defining and quantifying customer expectations
- Predicting service levels and managing corporate resources
- Planning and integrating sales and service
- Assessing and managing the company's competitive position

THE PRESSURES OF CONTINUING UPWARD REQUIREMENTS FOR QUALITY THROUGHOUT AN INCREASINGLY BROAD AND DIVERSE AMERICAN AND GLOBAL ECONOMY

As these requirements for quality continue to increase, the escalating demands for capitalizing management leadership excellence in companies large and small reflect the increasing breadth and complexity of the American and global economy. The economy's business demands and competitive opportunities are abundantly apparent in the manufacturing sector—from cars and trucks to aircraft and information products. Similarly, the economy's business demands and competitive opportunities are clear in other industries—from finance to airlines, hotels, and retailers. These demands and opportunities are evident in biotechnology—consider the issues that have been discussed in connection with genetically modified foods onward—and in health care in all the dimensions of patient treatment. They have been recognized in e-business through its increasing exposure of customers to a growing breadth of offerings and channels. And these demands now also include, very importantly, more and more definitive emphasis on the use of quality principles and methods throughout education, technology, and medicine and increasingly in government, public administration, and the professional occupations. Moreover, they are for a far more expansive use of quality practices throughout business than was seen in the original applications in product manufacturing, which themselves continue to grow in scope and importance, not only in manufacturing but also in many other industries, as well as business services.

Among the many examples, consider just three demands for improved management and leadership that illustrate some of the considerations bearing on the character of the requirement for improved management and leadership:

- Much greater effectiveness in meeting the quality challenges of cutting-edge technology
- Much more effective digital quality management and related software
- Much better integration of the results and economics of quality with other key management activity business measures

These three requirements are discussed in detail in the following sections.

1. RAPIDLY INCREASING DEMANDS OF CUTTING-EDGE TECHNOLOGY

The rapidly increasing quality demands of new cutting-edge technology-based products and service are abundantly clear—from optical networks and telematics in cars and trucks to wireless-based consumer products and financial services. Such technology-based products are becoming commoditized frighteningly quickly. Companies that once could expect a year or more of market leadership from their investments in new products now see that shrink to a few months or even a few weeks. For companies with very high technology investments to be successful, it is becoming increasingly important that they develop processes that enable them to enjoy the cash flow return from their new products for a reasonable time while their competitors try to catch up.

The resulting demands for quicker and quicker ramp-ups of product launches are hugely dependent for their success on the development and use of quality systems disciplines and technologies that create shorter time cycles but nonetheless provide complete quality discipline to assure fully successful product launch customer performance. Recognizing and meeting this demand are becoming a basic key to accomplishing the significant time cycle reductions in product design and development, production, supplier establishment and integration, and distribution and service required by high-technology industries both in the United States and throughout the world.

2. MUCH MORE EFFECTIVE DIGITAL QUALITY MANAGEMENT AND RELATED SOFTWARE

The second of these demand and opportunity areas is greater effectiveness in focusing on the successful quality management of the all-important digital information technology that is the basis for the communication networks that are critical to business operations.

Companies have learned a great deal about the necessity for such effective quality management of digital electronic information technology from experience in their electronic data interchange (EDI) and ERP and Intranet software installations. They have become very practical about what it realistically takes to achieve strong, on-schedule, genuinely high return-on-investment results from digitized information without first having to pass through a period in which the primary output is that all one gets is more bad data faster than one got those data before.

Strong progress in software quality itself has been one of the important accomplishments of this situation, after the long and difficult period in which the user had to be the inspector of software products. However, the performance of complete digital information and communications installations still depends on the following issues:

- Planning and equipment
- Application and integration
- Schedule adherence and economics
- Successful use

Taken together, these performance issues are making this strong progress in software quality one of the key areas for management excellence leadership.

3. MUCH BETTER INTEGRATION OF THE RESULTS AND ECONOMICS OF QUALITY WITH OTHER KEY MANAGEMENT ACTIVITY MEASURES

The third demand and opportunity area involves the *economics* of quality, which is becoming an integral factor in the managerial activity-based cost accounting and performance reporting of companies. This area represents a striking evolution from what earlier was case-by-case or merely anecdotal reference to such quality cost measurements.

This integration of the economics of quality with other key management activity business measures means that twenty-first-century companies will be less and less restricted by the traditional accounting metrics in their top-level strategic planning for product and service improvement and genuine cost reduction. In the past they measured on a top-line basis the areas of operations, sales, production, and similar factors. However, they did not measure such activities as the cost of quality and/or delivering customer satisfaction.

This force for making the economics of quality integrated with other key performance measurements provides a significantly effective financial and management focus on quality improvement, which builds company strength.

An example is one of the United States' continually most successful companies, which also bears one of the oldest and most widely respected American brand names. It is Union Pacific, the largest company in one of the most complex American businesses—because of its scope of transportation and other markets and customers and its range of economic, environmental, and geographic considerations, along with its development, installation, and management of complex, leading-edge information technology networks.

Dick Davidson, Union Pacific's chairman and CEO, has long emphasized (through personal, knowledgeable, and hands-on leadership) the importance of quality cost and its management as a center point for Union Pacific's service to its customers, investors, and many publics. He has also emphasized the company's effective, thorough, continually improving quality management. At Union Pacific's meetings with security analysts, the company's quality cost results and performance have been reported, together with other key business performance results. Similarly, at the chairman's quarterly meetings with senior management throughout the railroad, quality costs are thoroughly reviewed and discussed as a major factor in discussing performance.

THE MANAGEMENT INNOVATION CHALLENGE OF QUALITY AND COMPLETE CUSTOMER VALUE SATISFACTION

To sustain and escalate growth and profitability, one of the major management leadership challenges and opportunities of a twenty-first-century company is capitalizing its management power in terms of quality. This power is necessary to create and implement management innovations to achieve the following goals:

- To make quality a key business customer–focused *center point* for relentlessly increasing revenue growth and competitive leadership in today's demanding markets
- To form an integrated, seamless company quality value *network* through customer, producer, and supplier relationships

- To achieve complete customer quality value *satisfaction*, which drives buyer loyalty
- To streamline quality *innovation* for product and service leadership, which is needed in fast-moving markets where products and services can be overwhelmed frighteningly quickly by strong global competition
- To accelerate sales and earnings growth by reducing quality *failure costs*
- To encourage organizationwide quality *enthusiasm* through the tools and resources that create quality improvement entrepreneurs
- To maximize the quality and effectiveness of *digital information technology systems* and the Internet
- To assure that quality is the company's *international business language*, reflecting the globalization of today's markets

CHAPTER 11

POWERING MANAGEMENT CAPITAL

ONE OF THE PRIMARY CHARACTERISTICS of the new twenty-first-century management model is its meaning and emphasis concerning innovation. This is characterized by the institutionalization of—and the infrastructure, e-frastructure, and integration for—constant management innovation. The reason for this is that today an important characteristic of a successful business innovation is that it also positions a company for the next innovation: It is not only an end in itself. In every industry, from silicon and steel to optics and genetics, it is also a necessary condition for connecting systematic product R&D throughout the entire company—not only focusing it on a central research laboratory—and enhancing the assurance of its timing and success.

Compared to the pacesetters—and as fundamentally important as it is—some companies have not yet recognized this. They do not fully understand that they have been blindsided, outclassed, and acquired by the competition, in many cases because they have not understood this management model. Many of the companies that have seen and worked with this model still have a way to go toward its full implementation.

There are seven key areas of this new power of management capital for integration of company resources, innovation in all those resources, and income growth through excelling the performance of competitors. These seven areas require action and know-how in terms of the following:

- Thorough understanding of the tectonic shift in the character of business investment in profit-driving assets and in the management model for successful utilization of these assets to achieve strong twenty-first-century business results
- Leadership with the necessary high degree of passion, populism, and disciplined responsibility—all for exorcising outworn twentieth-century management doctrines and replacing them with new and more powerful practices to meet these new opportunities and demands
- Systematic identification of the key opportunities for employing this new power of management capital and aggressive implementation
- Clear identification and effectiveness assurance of the key management capital channels for creating and delivering these results, including their digitization where appropriate
- Full understanding of the management capital tools and measurements that can be used to accomplish these results

- Effective management capital structuring, certainly including clear company and corporate governance, recognizing the role of intangible assets
- Consistent delivery of results for company stakeholders, including emphasis on the principle that the customer—not Wall Street—delivers a company's income

Management capital is a business's overarching theme for capitalizing the management power for effectively recognizing, developing, accumulating, deploying, and measuring the capacity and effectiveness of a company's total resources—soft as well as hard—within the infrastructure and e-frastructure of the leadership, the people, and the processes for sustaining and accelerating profitable growth. It is energized by implementing and relentlessly increasing product, service, and other business values for customers and key company stakeholders and relentlessly emphasizing constant business management innovation to achieve the competitive leadership that makes this possible.

Its focus is on converging the opportunistic growth strength once thought of as New Economy with the fiscal responsibility of Old Economy discipline.

Its implementation recognizes the importance of identifying and overcoming the backward creep, disconnects, and failure costs that can be obscured by a strong business period, by outmoded standards, or by trying to blow through a weak and uncertain business period. Its emphasis is on the business network culture, whose defining characteristic is the speed of successful results. Its environment is one of open communications that develops the creativity of individual job entrepreneurs throughout the organization.

Finally, its constant emphasis is on effectively accumulating, innovating, and using management capital to sustain and accelerate company business growth and profitability in today's economic environment of great opportunity and brutally demanding competition.

Index

A
Acer, 78
Actions for growth, 39
Alignment:
　of business objectives, 164
　performance management and, 164
　of quality value in organization, 179–182
Alliances, 77
　for competitive leadership, 173–174
　growth management affected by strategic, 77–78
Amazon.com, 12, 32, 80
Ambiguity, 98
Analysis phase (of business physical), 107–108
Annual operating plan, 163, 164
Appraisal, 117
Asset monetization, 82
Assets:
　changing concepts about, 26–28, 31
　management of, 168–169
　soft, 137
Attention span, limited management, 101–103
Attitude, management capital, 96, 128
Attitudes, management innovation, 24–33
　on company's productive and marketing capacities, 26–28

Attitudes, management innovation (*Cont.*):
　on sustaining growth, 25–26
Automotive industry, 21, 77, 173

B
"Backward creep," 66, 93–94
Baldrige Award, 69
Banking, business failure costs in, 119
Bayer, 79
Best practices, 38, 142–143, 146–147
Blindsiding the competition, 11, 145–149
　human resources example of, 147–149
　with information management, 148, 150–152
　product development example of, 146–147
Boundaryless organizations, 10
Brand name, 9, 87
Business effective capability, 79
Business failure costs, 52, 82, 115–125
　hardware and software information systems example, 121–125
　and lost opportunity costs, 115–116
　management of, 120–121
　opportunities created by structuring, 117–120
　scope of, 116–117

Business growth, 3–16
  character of leadership for, 9–11
  drivers of, 12–14
  and integration of IT and management processes, 11–12
  management innovation for, 14–16
  new leadership/management models for, 6–7
  and quality of management, 7–9
  and quality of productivity, 5–6
  sustaining, 4–5
Business leadership capability, 79
Business management innovation, 19–34
  for business growth, 14–16
  challenge of, 22–24
  changing attitudes about, 24–33
  and corporate character, 65–70
  economic effects of, 19–20
  emphasis on, 159–160, 169, 170
  global business impact of, 67–70
  implementation of, 33–34
  in Japanese economy, 20–22
  quality challenge to, 187–188
  and quality of management, 47–50
  relentless, 129
  and systems effectiveness, 129
Business model focus, 162
Business objectives alignment, 164
The business physical, 92, 107–112
  analysis phase, 107–108
  construction phase, 109–111
  financial results and ROI, 110–112
  planning phase, 108–109
Business planning, 163
Business Week, 181
Buying volume, 87

C

Character, corporate (*see* Corporate character)
Cisco, 79
Clarity, 102
College of William and Mary, 30
Commodity use stage (of product development cycle), 144
Communication, 7, 33, 40, 71
Competence, 137
Competitive leadership, 137–153, 157–174
  blindsiding for, 145–149
  business model focus for, 162
  characteristics of, 137–140, 161–174
  company culture emphasis for, 160
  and corporate character, 60–61

Competitive leadership (*Cont.*):
  customer value emphasis for, 158
  dimensions of, 157–160
  environment for, 170–171
  goals establishment for, 165, 168–169
  implementation and innovation for, 169, 170
  importance of short-term goals for, 172
  information management for, 148, 150, 152
  integration of, 152–153
  invisible value creation for, 141–142
  management innovation emphasis for, 159–160
  materializing the intangibles for, 142–145
  operating cost emphasis for, 158–159
  organization flexibility and training for, 171–172
  partnerships and alliances for, 173–174
  senior management involvement in, 161–162
  total resource use structure for, 162–167
  visible value creation for, 140–141
Connected planning, 102
Consistency of improvement, 102, 103
Conspicuous consumption stage (of product development cycle), 144
Construction phase (of business physical), 109–111
Consumer goods organizations, management disconnects in, 104–105
Cooperation, 78
Corporate character, 59–72
  and competitive leadership, 60–61
  elements of, 70–72
  examples of, 61–62
  and global business impact of management innovation, 67–70
  and management innovation, 65–68
  and "signature" improvement practices, 62–65
  system impacts of, 128
Cost reduction, 94–96
Costs:
  business failure (*see* Business failure costs)
  fixed, 4–5
  operating, 53, 158–159
Creativity, 7
Culture, company:
  and company character, 59
  and company growth, 39
  for improvement, 71
  of superior performance, 160
Cummins Engine, 61, 140

Customer satisfaction, 4, 51, 177–188
  competitive leadership through, 158
  as competitive opportunity, 81
  emphasis on quality and, 178–179
  example of strategic quality management for, 182–184
  importance of, 6
  management innovation challenge of quality and, 187–188
  and market alignment focus on quality value, 179–180
  market power of, 177–178
  and organizational alignment of quality value, 181–182
  rising quality requirements for global, 184–187
  and signature improvement practices, 63, 64
  at Southwest Airlines, 62
Customer value, 66–67
Customers:
  dissatisfaction of, 85
  expectations of, 51
  feedback from, 87
  leadership focusing on, 10
  relationships with, 46–47
  understanding/respecting/responding to, 138–139

D
Daimler-Chrysler, 77
Davidson, Dick, 61, 117, 187
Dealer feedback, 87
Decentralization, 53
Defect reduction, 179
Delayering, 10
Dell Computer, 9, 11, 23, 29, 32
Deregulation, 76
Diffusion of responsibility, 59
Digital quality management, 186
Direct-to-customer, 11
Discipline, quality-of-management, 115
Disciplined responsibility, 41–42, 71, 106, 165, 168
Disconnect effect, 99, 100
Disconnects, management (*see* Management disconnects)
Disney, 30
Dollar exchange, 76
Dow-Jones Index, 19, 61
Drivers of business growth, 12–14
DuPont, 79

E
E-Bay, 9, 12, 25, 32, 80, 85
E-business, 12, 80
E-commerce, 12, 80
E-frastructure, 8
E-Superstore, 86
E-technology, opportunities in, 83–87
  malls and exchanges, 86–87
  manufacturing and production, 83–84
  marketing and sales, 84–85
  product development networks, 87
  supply management, 85–86
Economy:
  management innovation effects on, 19–20
  management *vs.*, 60
Effectiveness, systems (*see* Systems effectiveness)
800-pound gorilla, 177
Employees:
  dissatisfaction of, 47
  effectiveness of, 65–66
  empowerment of, 63, 64
  training of, 53, 97–98
Environment:
  as competitive opportunity, 82
  for individual improvement entrepreneurship, 40
  of positive attitudes and opportunistic involvement, 170–171
Equity indicators, 19
Exchanges, 86–87
External failure costs, 117

F
Fact-based quality of management, 46–47
Failure costs, business (*see* Business failure costs)
Fayol, Henri, 69
Federal Reserve Bank, 27
Feedback, 87
Finance, business failure costs in, 119
Finance-based improvement investment, 54
Financial capital, 7–8, 53
Financial results (of business physical), 110–112
"Firewall" protection, 87
Fireworks displays, 53, 97
Fixed costs, 4–5
Flexibility, organizational, 7, 76, 171–172
Ford, 77
Fuji Heavy Industries, 77
Functional use stage (of product development cycle), 144

G

Gantt, Henry, 69
Garten, Jeffrey, 181
General Electric (GE), 8, 10–11, 15, 23, 29, 32, 61, 79, 181
General Motors, 77
"General-purpose" technology, 12–14
General Systems, 121
Georgia Institute of Technology, 30
Germany, 69
Global economy:
    impact of management innovation on, 67–70
    rising quality requirements for, 184–187
Global expansion, 81
Global knowledge base, 62
Global market:
    growth management affected by, 75–76
    growth sustained in, 44–50
Globalization, 76
"GM Group," 77
Goals:
    establishment of, 165, 168–169
    short-term, 172
"Gods of management," 20
Greenspan, Alan, 12
Growth, business (see Business growth)
Growth management, 75–87
    global market affecting, 75–76
    improvement imperative in, 80–82
    Internet opportunities for, 83–87
    and market leader demands, 79–80
    strategic alliances affecting, 77–78
    technology affecting, 78–79

H

Hands-on focus, 71
Health care organizations:
    management disconnects in, 104–105
    systems effectiveness in, 131–133
Hidden organizations, 99–103, 118, 121
Hierarchy of ownership, 78
Hitachi, 21
Honda Motor Co., 21, 77
Human bridges, 126–128
Human resources, 47, 53, 98, 147–149

I

IBM, 9, 11, 23, 25, 32, 69, 78
"Imperial CEO," 23
Implementation:
    of business management innovation, 33–34
    emphasis on, 169, 170

Information management, 148, 150, 152
Information systems, 121–125
Information technology, 11–12
Information technology management, 81–82
Innovation (see Business management innovation)
Innovation management process flow, 67, 68
Innovation stage (of product development cycle), 144
Integrated systems networks, 124, 125
Intel, 8, 11, 32, 140
Intellectual content, 137
Internal failure costs, 117
Internet, 70
    as business model, 52
    competitive advantage with, 78–79
    as driver of business growth, 13
    "e-frastructure" of, 8
    and emphasis on quality value, 180
    growth management opportunities on, 83–87
    as management and consumer self-service, 75–76
    and management innovation, 70
    supply-chain network on, 29
Invisible hand, 5
Invisible value creation, 141–142, 152
Isuzu Motor Co., 77

J

Japan, 173
    business innovations from, 69
    business management innovation in, 20–22
    consumer electronics leadership of, 79
    equity indicator in, 19
Just-in-time management, 20

K

Knowledge base, 62
Komatsu, 21

L

Launch time, 129–130
Leadership:
    for business growth, 9–11
    competitive (see Competitive leadership)
    extending, 139
    needed to fix management disconnects, 105–106
    new business growth models of, 6–7
Limited management attention span, 101–103
Lost opportunity costs, 115–116
Loyalty, 66

M

Malls, 86–87
Management:
   of business failure costs, 120–125
   economy *vs.*, 60
   growth (*see* Growth management)
   new business growth models of, 6–7
   quality of (*see* Quality of management)
Management capital, 30–34
   employee involvement/empowerment supported by, 63, 64
   factors of, 32–33
   as foundation guidelines, 59–60
   implementation of, 33–34
   key areas for, 191–192
   and supervisors' changing role, 63, 65
Management capital attitude, 96, 128
Management capital leadership capability, 133
Management disconnects, 80, 91–112
   and "backward creep," 93–94
   and business physical, 107–112
   and cost reduction, 94–96
   in health care/consumer goods organizations, 104–105
   hidden organizations created by, 99–103
   premises for action on, 92–93
   problems at companies with, 97–99
   quality of leadership needed to fix, 105–106
   recognizing opportunities in, 91–92
   and slash-and-burn techniques, 96–97
   from transactional services to manufacturing, 103–104
Management doctrines, worn-out, 49, 51–54
Management innovation (*see* Business management innovation)
Management systems, 9
Manufacturing:
   business failure costs in, 119
   disconnects from transactional services to, 103–104
   e-technology opportunities in, 83–84
Market alignment, 179–180
Market leader demands, 79–80
Market power, 177–178
Marketing, e-technology opportunities in, 53, 84–85
Marketing capacities, 26–28
Markets, attitudes on new, 25–26
Materializing the intangibles, 142–145
Matrix I process, 164, 166
Matrix II process, 164, 166
Matsushita, 21
Mead, Dana, 62, 120
Measurement, 11, 14–15
Microsoft, 171
Morita, Mr., 20
Motivation, 39, 47
Multidimensional integrated management foundation, 52–53

N

National Cash Register, 69
"Natural" product development cycle, 143–145
Nestle, 62
Networking, 7, 59, 78
New York Times, 23
"Nickel-and-dimed," 99
Nikkei 225 Index, 19, 21
Nokia, 25, 32

O

Objectives, 140
Ohno, Mr., 20
One-or-two-or-out market leadership, 10
Openness, 40
Operating costs, 53, 158–159
Operational value, 32
Operationalizing new concepts, 28–30
Operations survey, 63
Opportunities:
   attitudes on new business, 25–26
   costs of lost, 115–116
   created by structuring business failure costs, 117–120
   in management disconnects, 91–92
Organizational alignment, 181–182
Organizational flexibility and training, 171–172
Ownership, 40

P

Pacesetter companies, 8–9, 9–11
"Painting the bridge" approach, 62–63
Partnerships, 11, 173–174
Passion, 39–40, 71, 106, 165
Patterson, William, 69
Perceived quality, 179
Perceived value, 16
Performance management and alignment, 164
Personal computers, 78
Personal ownership, 40
Physical assets, 7–8
Planning, 163

Planning phase (of business physical), 108–109
Populism, 40–41, 71, 106, 165
Prevention, 118
Pricing, product, 122
Prioritization of improvements, 51
Problem solving, 11
Product development cycle, 61, 129–130
   blindsiding example for, 146–147
   management of, 145
   "natural," 143–145
Product development management systems, 104
Product development networks, 87
Product development resources, 122
Product innovation, 82
Product technology capability, 79
Production, e-technology opportunities in, 83–84
Productivity, 5–6, 26–28
Promotion of company, 139–140
"Pull" manufacturing, 13, 83–84
"Push" manufacturing, 13, 84

Q
Quality:
   as competitive opportunity, 82
   and customer satisfaction, 4, 178–188
   of leadership needed, 105–106
   perceived, 179
   of productivity, 5–6
Quality cost initiative, 15
Quality management:
   integration of results and economics of, 186–187
   strategic, 182–184
Quality management software, 186
Quality of management, 37–55
   company growth sustained with, 38–39
   and disciplined responsibility, 41–42
   example of, 44–50
   fact-based, 46–47
   key channels of, 43–44
   and momentum for innovation, 47–50
   and passion, 39–40
   and populism, 40–41
   recognizing importance of, 7–9
   and worn-out management doctrines, 49, 51–54
Quality-of-management discipline, 115
Quality value, 6

R
Renault, 77
Resources, total use of, 21, 96, 120, 162–167, 164, 166

Return on investment (ROI), 14–15, 110–112
Risk management, 82
Roadblocks to growth, 39
ROI (*see* Return on investment)

S
Sales:
   business failure costs as percent of, 122, 123
   e-technology opportunities in, 84–85
   systems effectiveness in, 133
Sales growth, 133
Schumpeter, Joseph, 67, 68
Scope (of business failure costs), 116–117
Self service, 75–76, 85
Senior management involvement, 161–162
Service innovation, 82
Services, emphasis on, 11
Short-term goals, 172
"Signature" improvement practices, 62–65
"Signature" management systems, 61–62
Six sigma initiative, 15, 181
Slash-and-burn techniques, 96–97, 159
Sloan, Alfred P., 69
Smith, Adam, 5
Smith, John F., Jr., 77
Soft-asset capabilities, 137
Solso, Tim, 61
Sony, 21
Southwest Airlines, 62
Strategic alliances, 77–78
Strategic planning, 163
Strategic quality management, 182–184
Summers, Lawrence, 67
Supervisors, 63, 65
Supply management, 82, 85–86, 104
Suzuki Motor Co., 77
Systematic analysis, 39
Systematic integration, 11
Systematic management action, 59
Systematizing management innovation, 23–24
Systems effectiveness, 126–133, 129–131
   automotive manufacturing example of, 129–131
   health care facility example of, 131–133
   human bridges *vs.*, 126–128
   and management innovation, 129
   sales growth integration with growth of, 133

T
Taylor, Frederick, 69
Team-based operation growth, 148, 149

INDEX

Teamwork, 51
Technology:
  application of, 66
  competitive advantage with, 78–79
  as driver of business growth, 12–14
  growth management affected by, 78–79
  increasing demands of cutting-edge, 185
  integration of leadership with, 12
Tenneco, 62, 120, 121
Time cycle compression, 81
Timing, 59
Toshiba, 21
Total quality management, 11, 15, 30, 31, 181
Total resource use, 162–167
Toyoda, Dr., 20
Toyota, 11, 20–21
Toyota Motor Co., 77
Trade barriers, 76
Trade Xchange, 77
Training, 47, 171–172
Trust, 40

U
Union Pacific, 8, 11, 15, 23, 32, 61, 117, 187
United States, business growth in, 69
U.S. Treasury bonds, 76

V
Visible value creation, 140–141, 152
Volume, buying, 87

W
Wal-Mart, 8, 29, 32, 86
Walsh, Mike, 62, 120
Watson, Thomas, 69
Westinghouse, 11
"Winner-takes-all" business environment, 80
Work flow, 11
Work-out initiative, 15
Working patterns, 54

X
Xerox, 79

Y
Yahoo, 85